THE ART OF DAVID DABYDEEN

THE ART OF DAVID DABYDEEN

Edited by Kevin Grant

PEEPAL TREE

First published in Great Britain in 1997
Peepal Tree Press Ltd
17 King's Avenue
Leeds LS6 1QS
England

ISBN 1 900715 10 4

ACKNOWLEDGEMENTS

I am grateful to the editors of *Kunapipi*, *Ariel* and *The Journal of West Indian Literature* for permission to reprint articles by Benita Parry, Margery Fee, Frank Birbalsingh and Wolfgang Binder.

CONTENTS

PREFACE

This collection of essays is one of a series planned on contemporary British/Caribbean writers: writers born in the Caribbean but now living in Britain. It is increasingly acknowledged that these writers contribute an immense richness, variety and vitality to contemporary literatures in English, regularly winning major international prizes, from the Nobel to the Booker.

However, Black British literature is by no means a modern phenomenon. As early as the eighteenth century, slave narratives and autobiographies were published in Britain by writers such as Olaudah Equiano, Ignatius Sancho, Ottobah Cugoano and Ukawsaw Gronniosaw. These writers sought to assert the humanity of the African, unrecognised by a society that largely perceived Blacks as little better than wild animals.

The majority of English literature from the seventeenth century to the present day has perpetuated this perception. As David Dabydeen himself has pointed out, "black people have been fodder for white conceptualisation." Their social and historical realities ignored or denied, Blacks have been portrayed as variously evil, foolish, savage or exotic.

The first wave of immigrant writers in the 1950s sought to dispel such notions of 'otherness'. Dabydeen has described writers such as Sam Selvon, V S Naipaul, Wilson Harris and George Lamming as "missionaries in reverse", with a duty to reveal their humanity to an ignorant British society. This Caribbean literature was more than an attempt to voice the complex cultural experiences of the immigrant. It was an act of self-definition.

David Dabydeen is one of the leading voices of the second wave of immigrant writers. Sent to England from Guyana in 1969, in Care for three years before gaining a place at Cambridge University, he has occupied the perfect position from which to examine the plurality of the Caribbean experience. Slavery, cultural denigration, migration, dislocation and psychic division are recurring themes in his work.

More strikingly, Dabydeen is unique in being the only poet to employ Guyanese rural English in his work. Control of language is a dominant feature of imperial oppression, and only the creation of a postcolonial voice can overthrow such power. Dabydeen's startlingly innovative form shuns conventional English grammar in favour of a Creole voice infinitely more powerful in expressing the complexities of the Caribbean experience.

Dabydeen's writings differ markedly from his predecessors in that he seeks to mask rather than reveal self, and it is this process of concealment that Mark McWatt elucidates in the opening chapter on *Slave Song*. He describes Dabydeen's use of multiple masks to suggest the complexity of the West Indian identity. The poems themselves, the critical notes on each poem, the translation of each poem into Standard English, and the volume's illustrations create several alternative 'texts' which interact to simultaneously project and conceal the persona of the poet.

Sarah Lawson Welsh takes up Mark McWatt's line of analysis when she argues that *Slave Song's* incorporation of Standard English translations and an Eurocentric critical apparatus somewhat tames the energy and radicalism of the poems. However, she goes further, suggesting that the translations and notes form an integral part of the text. Dabydeen's role as critic is just another in a series of masks.

Benita Parry's essay focuses on Dabydeen's use of Creole and Cambridge English in his search for a language that will speak the Guyanese history and landscape. His ambition to 'speak' for the historically muted is a fiction, she argues, for he must reinvent the speech and fantasies of the slaves and canecutters. *Slave Song* and *Coolie Odyssey* are ultimately rewritings of the

West's master narrative, addressing the postcolonial condition. As poetry that subverts Standard English, however, it has the capacity to alter the Eurocentric consciousness of its audience.

Margery Fee turns her attention to Dabydeen's first work of fiction, the clearly autobiographical, *The Intended.* Its theme of a young Guyanese immigrant's quest for an identity acceptable to the British establishment is undercut by the 'messiness' of the narrative structure, revealing the author's ultimate allegiance to his West Indian identity, despite his uncertain and shifting loyalties. The novel is 'folked up', argues Fee, turning the reader away from the hero's attempts to become white and towards his subsequent struggle to become black. This shift transforms the novel into a postcolonial allegory, rejecting the 'birdcage' of Standard English, clarity, order and homogenous identity in favour of the celebration of an apparently haphazard Creole and a multifaceted identity.

The fractured structure of *The Intended* is also the focus for Benita Parry's second essay. The narrator seeks to redefine his identity and liberate himself from a colonial condition by writing the oppressor's language. Yet the fracturing of the narrative structure highlights the fact that such historical and cultural amnesia is impossible. Like the visionary Joseph, the narrative is multilocated, dispersed, and creolized, points out Parry, undercutting the narrator's attempts to create a Standard English text and a homogenous self.

The central theme of *Disappearance*, Dabydeen's second novel, is a search for the elusive quality that is Englishness, Jean Popeau asserts. The Guyanese engineer who attempts, through science, to protect an English village from the ravages of the sea, also seeks his own colonial roots, but both prove illusive. It is perhaps only Mrs. Rutherford, with her collection of African masks, who can be perceived as a truly postcolonial figure, both self and other, through her capacity for empathy. The narrator, in his attempts to control and rationalise, is left with an identity that

seeks to banish the 'other', to banish all traces of the darkness of
his colonial past.

Mark McWatt examines both novels in an attempt to show how
Dabydeen, in his dual role as academic and writer, brings together postcolonial theory and West Indian literature. Dabydeen
self-consciously employs postcolonial counter-discursive techniques in his writing, destabilizing the dominant discourse. In
The Intended, Joseph's visionary reading of Conrad's *Heart of
Darkness* stands as a counter-discursive ploy, undercutting the assumed marginality of the black, illiterate 'other'. Similarly,
Marlow's journey up the Congo is reduced to a sleazy fairground
ride. In *Disappearance*, the narrator is free to question the authority of the books on Mrs. Rutherford's shelf. With no allegiance to
Eurocentric values and no sense of cultural purity in relation to
his native Guyana, he can furnish the books with the chaos of
possibility, of counter-discourse. Yet such 'literary gamesmanship'
and authorial intrusions are in danger of robbing the narrator of
his life, warns McWatt, rendering the postcolonial novel as little
more than a means of making a theoretical point.

Mario Relich sees Dabydeen's writing as essentially the drama-
tization of an inner conflict. In *Slave Song* and *Coolie Odyssey*
Dabydeen draws attention to his own alienation and psychic divisions, a conflict inherent in a West Indian identity torn between
the cultures and values of its ancestors and those of the colonial
exploiters. In *The Intended*, the narrator provides a triple perspective on his experiences, drawing distinctions between a
childhood in Guyana, an adolescence in Balham and an adulthood
as a university student. The childhood experiences are not described chronologically and disrupt the narrative of the adolescent experiences, and this rupture between past and present is
reflected in the way the language slips from adult English to
childhood Creole. These narrative techniques dramatically convey
the narrator's sense of psychic disorientation. Ultimately his faith
in words, and his acceptance of the oral culture of Guyana, re-

leases the narrator's creative power, while Joseph succumbs to the lure of the media and finds only nothingness. The narrator's final rejection of an identity resulting from neo-colonial stereotyping confirms *The Intended* as a novel subversive about British culture.

In the final essay, Karen McIntyre deals with Dabydeen's most accomplished writing so far, the epic poem, *Turner*. McIntyre seeks to show how *Turner* records the imaginative and timeless struggle for creativity untainted by colonialism, negotiating the problems of identity and history in its passage towards creative decolonisation; that is, the dismantling of European authority and the creation of an independent identity. This is achieved through Dabydeen's use of a variety of alternative, competing selves or 'Turners', combating the notion of homogenous identity. The subject of Turner's painting, the shackling and drowning of African slaves, had previously been relegated to a footnote. By revisioning the submerged African head, giving it a body and a biography, Dabydeen elevates this footnote, which becomes a lost history and culture, 'plugging' the 'holes' in Western versions of colonial history. Rather than a purely necrophilial engagement with the past, resulting in a stale creation, or stillbirth, Dabydeen employs what McIntyre terms creative necrophilia, so that creativity is *still*born.

The most striking aspect of David Dabydeen's work is its concern with language and its power to redeem. From the "barbaric energy" within the brokenness of Creole in *Slave Song*, to the sensuous and lyrical beauty of the English language in *Turner*, there is a sense of mischievous playfulness in Dabydeen's attempts to pervert the language, to stretch it to its limits. In this way, Black British literature in general, and the work of Dabydeen in particular, has provided a vivid insight into the complex and contradictory nature of the Caribbean identity, together with novel and illuminating perspectives on English society and culture. Perhaps most importantly it has succeeded in breaking down and transcending the Eurocentric canons of Empire. Without doubt it has rejuvenated English literature, and enriched those it has touched.

CHAPTER I

HIS TRUE-TRUE FACE: MASKING AND REVELATION
IN DAVID DABYDEEN'S *SLAVE SONG*

MARK MCWATT

The writings of David Dabydeen, whether poetry, prose fiction or autobiographical sketches, provide an interesting example of the creative use of the technique of masking. The writer/narrator/poetic persona uses multiple masks in order both to suggest the complexity of the identity of the West Indian East Indian, and also, one suspects, to protect certain aspects of self from the kind of 'knowing' described by Lamming as his reason for the retreat into "the castle of my skin". It is interesting that the technique of masking which is used defensively – to discourage certain facile readings of the text of the 'self' – appears to be more prevalent in those West Indian writers (Lamming, Naipaul, Dabydeen) who seem most aware of the non-West Indian contexts in which they live and write. Other writers, such as Walcott, Brathwaite and Lovelace, use the technique of masking differently, and certainly less self-consciously.

What is interesting about the writing of Dabydeen is that he persistently calls attention to the technique of masking in his work, to the point where the technique itself assumes a part of the burden of meaning and comments on or interrogates other aspects of the work. This is perhaps best observed in *Slave Song*,[1] Dabydeen's first volume of poetry. In this work we are presented with fourteen poems, each of which is itself a carefully constructed mask by means of which the poetic persona inhabits the men and women – slaves and indentured labourers – who worked the sugar lands of Guyana; but these poems, in raw Guyanese Creole, are only part of the text of *Slave Song*. There is a critical/ explanatory note on each poem – often including a brief glossary of the more difficult words and expressions as well as a "translation" of the poem into standard English. There are also a number of illustrations: historical prints of slave and plantation life which also become part of the technique of multiple masking that controls the meaning and effect of the work as a whole.

This technique sets up several different loci of authority within the volume, several different 'texts': there is the poem itself with its vigorous Creole voice conveying aspects of lived experience and the feelings and imagination of the slave or peasant in a very powerful way. This vivid mask of suffering, of 'pure' energy and emotion, is then modified for the reader first by the mask of the critic/commentator and then by the mask of the translator, both insisting, it seems, on a different 'purity', of perspective and of expression. It is equally true, on the other hand, that the emotional integrity of the dialect voice of the poem diminishes the authority of note and of translation. The reader is thus left with a curious sensation of dislocation as the different aspects of the text suffer a partial eclipse or erasure when juxtaposed and allowed to interact. This is made clear when we sample the different levels of text pertaining to the title poem. First a stanza and refrain from the poem 'Slave Song':

> Whip me till me bleed
> Till me beg.
> Tell me how me hanimal
> African orang-utan
> Tell me how me cannibal
> Fit fo slata fit fo hang.

Slice waan lip out
Waan ear an waan leg –
Bu yu caan stap me cack dippin in de honeypot
Drippin at de tip an happy as a hottentot!

It is one thing for the critic, in a paper such as this, to attempt a critical interpretation of this passage, and something else entirely to find that the job has already been done for him by the poet – or has it? Here is part of the "note" on *Slave Song*:

> The slave addresses his Master (mentally of course). He asserts his manhood, his dignity and his instinct for survival through his surreptitious lust for the white woman, his Mistress . . . On one level his lust is obscene and revengeful: he can cuckold his Master by mentally degrading his Master's wife, dragging her down to his level of existence; that is he can 'Africanize' her ('totempole her cunt', 'leave his teeth mark like a tattoo on her throat' – lines 32-3). He boasts that he can really act out the role of a cannibal (designated to him – line 15 – by his white superiors) by gaining life at her expense. But such lust is also life-giving in a more poignant way . . .

We will immediately recognize this as the kind of critical interpretation of poetry that we all do – it is part of the way we make our living; yet we feel somewhat uneasy, perhaps, when the poet deliberately puts on this mask and grins at us from behind it. It seems mockingly to invite us to criticize the criticism, along with the poem, and in fact forces us to recognize the inevitable gap – which our critical commentary tends to paper over – between the creative utterance and the critical interpretation. Here, for instance, we are forced to reflect on whether the slave's cry, "Tell me how me cannibal/Fit fo slata fit fo hang", can really be interpreted as the somewhat sophisticated boast of gaining life at the

white woman's expense that the critical mask offers us in the
"note".

By interpreting the poem, the "note" distances and changes it,
and this is one of the things we are forced to recognize as we con-
template the interaction of the masks of poet/slave and critic. It
also makes the reader acutely aware of criticism as a mask: by
'putting the critic on', the poet is poking fun at the critic and his
techniques, as well as calling into question the integrity of the
text. In the case of *Slave Song*, what is the text? Where are its
limits and boundaries? If poem and critical note tend towards the
erasure or disintegration of each other, where does one turn to
find the locus of significance or meaning within the whole thing?
What is the true face behind the different masks? Dabydeen himself has commented on the notes to the poems in *Slave Song*, and
in fact he has upset some readers, by dismissing the thing as a
joke:

> Many of the notes are spoof notes: they are almost saying
> that I want to be the critic as well as the poet . . . it's just
> that I felt I would do the whole lot, and the poems would al-
> most be minimalist poems. What mattered were not just the
> poems, but the notes to the poems. None of the poems uses
> the word "I"; one inhabits a series of masks, and the notes
> were my way of saying, "Look, I am just rendering history;
> look, I am the critic." Of course this is a complete illusion,
> a farce.[2]

But this raises the question of how seriously one must take
these remarks; might they not simply be the features of yet another mask? As a matter of fact some of the language towards the
end of the quote above is perhaps revealing: Note the use of 'I'
and 'one'. His remark that none of the poems use the word 'I', immediately followed by his reference to himself as 'one' indicate a
certain sensitivity about the self, perhaps; about revealing too

much of the true face behind the masks. Then, in the direct speech that follows, he uses the personal pronoun twice, but each represents a separate mask: "Look, I am just rendering history (poem); look, I am the critic (note)". Perhaps this is the only 'safe' way in which the "I" can be used – to inhabit carefully defined masks. This would help explain the urge to pass the whole complex mechanism off as a joke; it is another way of preserving and protecting the self, the true-true face.

In another section of the interview quoted above, Dabydeen in fact reveals that his concern with the notes is much more than a joke. "I am concerned," he says, "about the critical business that thrives upon the expression of poverty and dispossession, which is what the Caribbean voice ultimately is."[3] This confirms that the poet is calling attention to the somewhat sinister role of the critic and to whose side he is really on when the world is seen in terms of the opposition between slave and master, black and white, colony and metropole. You will observe in the note to 'Slave Song' quoted above that when the critic-mask quotes lines from the poem in illustration of his argument, he quotes the lines from the sanitized translation rather than from the creole language of the poem itself ("totempole her cunt, leave his teeth marks like a tattoo on her throat" – rather than "totempole she puss, leff yu teetmark like a tattoo in she troat!"). This subtle but deliberate departure from normal critical practice when quoting puts the critic firmly in the camp of master/white/metropole – showing that the critic knows on which side his bread is buttered, and vividly highlighting the political aspects of the relationship between creative artist and critic. Thus the mask of critic here, however it may conceal or protect certain sensitive aspects of the writer's 'self', also functions to reveal aspects of the nature and politics of criticism – and not only formal criticism, but ordinary reader-response as well; the technique of masking reveals the reader, at least as much as it conceals the writer.

Turning now to the mask of translation, here's how the passage quoted above from the poem 'Slave Song' is rendered by the translator-mask:

Whip me till I bleed/Till I beg./Tell me I'm an animal/An African orang-utan/Tell me I'm a cannibal/Fit only for slaughter or hanging/Slice one lip out
One ear and one leg –
But you can't stop my cock dipping in the honeypot,/
Dripping at the tip and happy as a hottentot!

What is immediately clear is the way in which the translation emasculates the poem; the power and authority of the poem (which even the critic-mask dutifully recognized) is subtly located in the authenticity of the Creole voice, in the desperate breath that carried the sounds, in the vital coarseness of the sexual threat in the refrain. Here in the translation, the poem's emotional power is tamed and trammelled, much like the "charter'd Thames" and "charter'd streets" of Blake's London, so that we find the translator identified very much with the oppressor, perpetrating a subtler form of the enthralment of the natural energies of the black man – the chain and the whip replaced by the measured and standardized language and tone. Note the way in which the wild, functional coarseness of the Creole refrain becomes simply obscene in this rendering.

Another accomplishment of these interacting masks within the volume is to displace or disguise the creative mind behind the entire contrivance. It is hard to believe in any close relationship – let alone complete identity – between the voice in the poems and those in the notes and translations; where then is the persona, the writer? If the technique of these multiple masks was intended to distract attention from the vulnerable self of the persona, then in a curious way it has failed: the reader is forced in the end, to be aware of the distractingly manipulative intelligence behind the work. When one reflects, for instance, that the simile "happy as a Hottentot", particularly when applied to a dripping penis, does not seem an image that would be native or natural either to the slave in Guyana or to the aloof translator, one is forced to glimpse a different persona, fleshed out perhaps by one's knowledge of David Dabydeen, the scholar of Africa and of eighteenth and nineteenth-century England, having mischievous fun at the expense of reader, critic and linguist.

Some of the techniques in *Slave Song* are reminiscent of Pope in the *Dunciad*,[4] and Dabydeen exhibits the same complex intellectual playfulness, though towards a different end. It is possible to see Dabydeen as conducting an elaborate postcolonial critique of traditional notions of the integrity of the text, of the relationship between text and critic, and of certain assumptions concerning the supremacy of standard forms of language. It is clear that the critic-mask, for all of its sophisticated use of language and the techniques of interpretation and explication, is constantly being interrogated by the recalcitrance of the language of the imagination as expressed in the dialect. At the same time, the attempt to defuse or detoxify the raw energy of the poetic voice calls into question the whole enterprise of literary criticism when applied across racial and socioeconomic divides such as those highlighted in this work.

Similarly, the translations offered convey not so much a clarification of the meaning and intent of the 'dialect-poet-mask' as an assertion or reassertion of the power relationships between users of standard and those who speak dialect. And here again the interference works both ways: the translator may feel that he is performing a service for the poem by making it more widely 'available', but the experience of the juxtaposition of poem and translation makes clear that what is available is a pale shadow of the real thing – the poem wearing a mask that makes it acceptable, but at the same time attenuates its power and effect. The poem, for its part, interrogates and subverts the translation

by its originality and energy. Dabydeen himself has pointed out
the power of the Creole:

> Creole has its own native strengths and you can convey cer-
> tain experiences very powerfully in a way that English could
> not be used . . . There's a kind of crudity in Creole – and my
> use of it was influenced not by living in a village in Guyana,
> but by [discovering] in Cambridge that Mediaeval [English]
> alliterative expression was beautifully barbaric, and this pro-
> voked memory of my native Creole, its "thew and sinew", its
> savage energy, its capacity for savage lyricism.[5]

This awareness of the power of the Creole, set alongside the
pallor of many of the translations, surely indicates the extent to
which we are involved, in this volume, in a game of masks intended to heighten our awareness of the power of poetry and dialect and to subvert any colonial assumptions we might have about
the superiority of English language and culture – of the 'text' of
English literature as primary and unassailable.

Another aspect of *Slave Song* worth mentioning in connection
with the use of masks is the half-dozen illustrations scattered
among the poems. These extend the technique of the multiple
masks in that they provide a curiously incongruous commentary
on the text(s), both visually and in terms of the strange disso-
nance between some of the pictures and their captions. Most of
these are engravings dating from the eighteenth or early nineteenth century and depicting aspects of slave and plantation life
in the Caribbean.[6] Apart from the historical resonance in these
pictures, which fits in well with the theme of slavery, they also
suggest a strangely vicarious mentality – looking at slave and
plantation life filtered through the preconceptions and prejudices
of white master which cause the images to be oddly stylized and
bereft of overt emotional content.

The picture of the slave tied to a wooden frame for execution is an example of this: the illustration is meant to seem factual, or rather, technical; the faces of the humans are devoid of feeling and the tone of the caption reinforces the mask of emotional detachment. But the illustration appears in Dabydeen's text opposite the poem 'Slave Song' that we have been examining above; and what we tend to see in this context is not so much an execution as a sexual defilement: the standing figure seems about to attack the genitals of the victim – it is a brutal rape or castration (it is unclear whether the figure is male or female), suggesting the punishment awaiting the slave in the poem for daring to dream of defiling the wife of his white master.

The illustration captioned simply: 'A piece of sugar cane' is in fact a piece of cane cut in longitudinal section to reveal infestation by some kind of worm or parasite; it is a horribly phallic image of pestilence and decay, and is juxtaposed with the poem 'The Canecutters' Song', where the canecutter is again dreaming of illicit sex with the white woman. Again the picture 'reads' like a sternly negative and minatory image not only of the consequences of the dream but of the whole life and livelihood of the canecutter.

There is a similar oddness in the picture captioned: 'A Female negro slave with a weight chained to her ankle': the chain is indeed fastened around the woman's ankle, but the weight is being placed by her on the side of her head. As with the poem/note/translation, the oddness of the image causes the observer to look behind the image itself and to speculate about the motives of the mind that created it. Again it is a question of the mask concealing or obscuring meaning while at the same time revealing aspects of the human agency behind/within it – a simultaneous attraction and repulsion akin perhaps to Walcott's reaction in 'A Far Cry From Africa', to the mixture of ancestral bloods within him. In any case this double movement indicates perfectly the relationship between blacks and white masters, between metropole and rural periphery and between the reader and the several masks in this work.

In the picture of the 'Suriname Planter in his Morning Dress' the caption masks the fact of the other human figure visible in the picture, that of the female slave that gives the planter his status, identity and worth, as she pours him a morning beverage in the background. This slave's nakedness above the waist also reveals, perhaps, something about the Suriname Planter, whose own masculine chest is glimpsed almost down to the waist. As with the other pictures the physical deployment of the bodies appears at the same time to be mysteriously suggestive and overtly revealing – as with all the other masks, the interest here is in what the image conceals as well as what it reveals.

Much of the effect of *Slave Song*, then, is to be found within the gaps between the various masks used to project/conceal the persona or the creative mind responsible for it. It has to do, as we have seen, with various aspects of and levels of textuality, with post-colonial criticism, with international games; but since *Slave Song* is the young poet's first publication, it may have to do as well with a natural diffidence, an uneasiness about the casual revelation of self by someone who has written elsewhere about his tough struggle to make it as a scholar and a writer among the Asian immigrants in London[7]. The apparatus of notes, translations and pictures has to do, too, with the necessity simply to contain and manage the enormous energy of the poetic voice from the Indian villages of Guyana – a voice hardly heard before, a compound and complex voice for whom the frail poet must serve as messenger, translator, apologist, explicator . . . It is a voice filled with the quality of 'dread', with accumulated animosity, with the desperate need for an audience. The masks are multiple channels for this voice and for the vital optimism of a poet who yearns to be all things for the sake of his people and for the sake of his art:

> . . . I do hope that I can be intensely Guyanese, or intensely Berbician, or English, or European. In other words, one has

the possibilities of inhabiting different masks intensely. I'm not just saying, take one mask, put it on, throw it away, then take another one . . .⁸

Notes

1   David Dabydeen, *Slave Song*, (Mundelstrup, Denmark: Dangaroo Press, 1984).

2   David Dabydeen, interviewed by Wolfgang Binder in *Journal of West Indian Literature*, Vol.3, No.2, September, 1989, p.75. Reproduced in this book.

3   *Ibid.*

4   Dabydeen, in a subsequent interview with Professor Frank Birbalsingh (in *Kunapipi*, Vol. X11, No.3, 1990) acknowledges the influence of Pope and Eliot on his footnoting. Reproduced in this book.

5   *Journal of West Indian Literature*, Interview, p.76.

6   One of them, that of the Suriname Planter, is by William Blake and, along with three of the others, from *Narrative of Five Years' Expedition against the Revolted Negroes of Suriname, in Guiana* (two vols. 1776).

7   See "From Care to Cambridge", an autobiographical piece by David Dabydeen in *Displaced Persons*, ed. Anna Rutherford, (Mundelstrup, Denmark: Dangaroo Press, 1988) pp. 137 - 147.

8   David Dabydeen, interviewed by Frank Birbalsingh in *Kunapipi*, *op. cit.*

CHAPTER II

EXPERIMENTS IN BROKENNESS: THE CREATIVE USE
OF CREOLE IN DAVID DABYDEEN'S *SLAVE SONG*

SARAH LAWSON WELSH

"an uncouth jargon [which] though English... I could com-
prehend little or nothing of..."
[Mrs Carmichael, the wife of a planter who spent the years
1820-25 with her husband in St Vincent & Trinidad].[1]

"Nothing can correct the radical depravity of this speech."
[Robert Southey, 'The New Testament in the Negro Tongue',
on the Surinam creole used in the Moravian Mission Bible,
1830].[2]

"It really was a pity that such intelligence and industry were
not devoted to some more useful object."
[Contemporary review of Trinidadian J.J. Thomas' pioneering
Creole Grammar of 1869.][3]

In a significant number of European travellers' accounts of their
visits or residence in the West Indies from the eighteenth century
onwards, creoles were figured as 'broken English', 'degenerate'
linguistic forms which conveniently reflected the alleged 'depravity' and 'uncivilized' or 'childlike' status of their speakers. This
chapter explores some of the permutations of brokenness as ex-

perimental linguistic medium, literary trope, historical and experimental paradigm and considers the creative potentialities of
these permutations as they are realized in *Slave Song*. The collection, as a whole, inscribes but also resists different readings of
brokenness; for example, Dabydeen writes in his introduction of
the brokenness of creole as a "naturally tragic language... no
doubt reflecting the brokenness and suffering of its original users
– African slaves and East Indian indentured labourers"[4]; however,
this concept of a doubled brokenness is resisted, in practice, by a
number of dominant and defiant voices in the poems, voices
which refuse to be broken (eg. 'Slave Song'), which are not beaten
or reduced to despair and which are markedly fluent rather than
faltering. *Slave Song* is also characterized by a certain formal and
generic 'brokenness' or unevenness, and the problematic relationship between the poems and the self-generated critical apparatus
which is included within the collection is analysed in this context.

The attitudes to West Indian creoles, with which the chapter
opened, are characteristic of a range of early accounts of creoles,
ranging from the famously ethnocentric writings of Edward Long[5]
and J.A. Froude[6], to the travel journals of British literary figures
such as Anthony Trollope and Charles Kingsley and the testimonies of a host of less well-known voices[7], especially in the nineteenth century. As examples of early colonialist discourse, they
demonstrate quite clearly how the West Indies and its linguistic
forms were selectively represented to Europe in the form of highly
polemical and ideologically-saturated accounts masquerading as
transparent or representative documents. However, as major de-
terminants of essentially negative popular attitudes to creoles
within and also outside of the West Indies, the damage they ex-
erted was both lasting and profound. Disturbingly, the unfamiliar-
ity of creole forms to many Western ears and the chronic
misunderstanding of their linguistic basis which characterized
such early accounts, still distinguish some accounts of creole use,

particularly in literary[8] and educational circles, even today. The tradition of according creoles – and black linguistic forms generally – an inferior, degenerate status and a childlike, simplified or comic image also owes much to dominant literary representations.

In America in the nineteenth and early twentieth centuries, such images were much augmented by the fictional depiction of 'Negro language' in novels such as Harriet Beecher Stowe's *Uncle Tom's Cabin* and Mark Twain's *Huckleberry Finn*. In Britain, the ethnographic fiction of writers such as Edgar Rice Burroughs, John Buchan and Henry Rider Haggard gave a more threatening, savage dimension to popular images of the black and his speech. Traces of such attitudes have survived well into our own century. For example, the Music Hall stereotype of the simplistic and sentimentalized 'singing Negro' was still publicly extant even as late as the 1960s, in the form of the 'blacked-up' minstrels of 'The Black and White Minstrel Show' in Britain. It is partly against this barrage of popular images and attitudes, with its long (and often decidedly murky) pedigree, and partly against the low esteem accorded to creoles by their own speakers[9,] that contemporary writers seeking to use creole have had to fight.

The creative use of creole is arguably always a political decision, and especially so when the speakers are diglossic or polydialectal, that is, they command more than one lect of a Caribbean language and have competence in the most standardized or acrolectal variety. Until relatively recently, there was little confluence between the linguistic study of creoles and the study of the potentialities of creoles as an expressive medium. Significantly, this interface has been most profitably explored by indigenous speakers such as John Rickford and Kamau Brathwaite, who re-appropriate creoles as the valid subject of linguistic study and of literary experimentation[10]. It is largely due to more accessible studies such as these that creoles have become more accurately understood and their creative potentialities fully tapped; however, there is still work to be done in this area.

As Dabydeen points out, "the potentiality for [creole] literature is very great indeed", for creole is "capable of expressing the full experience of its users which is a very deep one"[11]. The number of contemporary Caribbean or Black British poets utilizing creole in a creative capacity and demonstrating it to be a versatile medium, has increased dramatically in the last 15 years[12]. Significantly their work has also enabled a number of stereotypes surrounding the use of creole to be broken down; firstly, that it is employed primarily for comic effect; secondly, that it is an attempt merely to effect verisimilitude and thirdly, that it is the medium only of politicized protest poetry – often of the most mediocre kind. On the contrary, creole has proven a medium resourceful enough to encompass a range of poetic effects: lyrical, robust, dramatic and satiric among them.

The poems in Dabydeen's *Slave Song* are more than Browning-esque voice-portraits transferred to a Caribbean context – they are, as the title suggests, first and foremost songs: songs of resistance. Songs, as Burnett reminds us, were the Caribbean's first poems[13], an important locus of linguistic and communal resistance in slave populations on plantations throughout the Caribbean and North America. Dabydeen has spoken of the overall concept behind *Slave Song* as "in the title, slave and song, the contradiction between the two. What I wanted to show was the way of life that survived brilliantly and wickedly, mischievously and tragically, in spite of certain experiences of violence and brutality"[14]. The continued close relationship between music and word is one of the salient features of Caribbean poetry and in *Slave Song*, Dabydeen explores the creative potentialities of song in many forms and dimensions: work-song, call and response and choric forms, adapted folk song and bawdy, celebratory songs of domestic ritual, voice portraits of frustration and defiance, love-song and elegy.

However, as in Kamau Brathwaite's poetry, the music is present at the level of the language used as much as in the musical structures adopted and adapted to poetic forms. Dabydeen has described[15] the musical quality of *Slave Song* as one arising in part from his attempt to use talismanic words with a specifically Hindu notation. This imaginative attempt to assert the music and linguistic traces of a very different ancestry and cultural inheritance, feeding into and breaking through the adapted Guyanese creole which is his poetic medium in *Slave Song*, has been as significant as it has been unique. Whereas the Indo-Caribbean experience has been well documented in West Indian *fiction* by writers such as Sam Selvon, Dabydeen stands virtually alone in his attempt as *poet* to redress the balance of poetic material dealing with the Caribbean, which has hitherto been heavily weighted towards the *African* elements of Caribbean experience and cultural inheritance. However, his project as an *Indo*-Caribbean poet should not be seen as tokenist or marginal. *Slave Song* is important not only because of its fresh ethno-cultural perspective but also because of its experimental quality and the directness of its creole medium.

The robust defiance of many of Dabydeen's poems in this collection stand in sharp relief to the elegiac tone, the images of fragile cultural transfer and quietly atrophying Indian culture, which are central to Derek Walcott's depiction of an Indo-Caribbean community in 'The Saddhu of Couva'[16]. The dominant tone of *Slave Song*, as Benita Parry has pointed out, is rather, "overwhelmingly that of public protestation"[17], often combined, as in the title poem, with a celebratory and defiant sexuality. Yet amongst the more problematic poems[18] of "corrosive sexuality"[19] and "starkly pornographic experiences"[20], intervals of lyrical tenderness and poignant introspection are to be found. These moments are largely devoted to the study of the individual – and specifically in relation to another person, as in 'Men and Women'. Even 'Elegy', the one poem in the collection which is perhaps most akin to Walcott's imaging of cultural decay in its own charting of the demise of a particular rural way of life in Guyana, is transmuted through a voice-portrait which is highly personalized rather than generic. The fact that the resilience of *Slave Song* is drawn largely from the imaginative reconstruction and 'revocalization' rather than observation of contemporary Indo-Caribbean communities, has been well documented[21] but does not, I think, lessen the vigour and intensity of the poetry. *Slave Song* marks an important departure from and extension to the experimentation with musical forms of African origin in Caribbean poetry and has been one of the most innovative contributions to a growing body of creole poetry.

Creole is particularly suited to lyrical uses, as part of a directly personal and intense style. Unlike 'Standard English' it is an informal emotive language strongly associated with intimacy and group solidarity rather than distance or divisiveness amongst speakers, able to offer a refreshing directness in place of the abstraction of sophistication of 'Standard English'[22]. Jamaican poet James Berry makes lyrical use of creole as the quiet, almost reverential medium of intimacy between two people, conveying the tenderness and joy of lovemaking as a welcome release from poverty and pain in 'Style Freedom'[23]. The same reverential quality, tinged with regret, characterizes his first person monologue: 'Words of a Jamaican Laas Moment Them'[24]. Here the invocation of absolution is couched in almost Biblical images, of water, the mending of physical and spiritual brokenness and the washing away of sins:

> mek all the Island wash – wash away
> the mess of my shortcomings –
> all the brok-up things I did start.
> Mi doings did fall short too much.
> Mi ways did hurt mi wife too often.

In *Slave Song*, David Dabydeen's creole monologue, 'Men and Women' deals with similar subject-matter, as a Guyanese peasant returns in his old age to the wife he deserted many years earlier, filled with "the pain of remorse" at the hardships and suffering he helped to inflict on her young life. More complex than Berry's poem, 'Men and Women' is doubly poignant for its dual consideration of the pain of memory and the privations of old age and its charting of broken promises and aborted dreams. At the end of the poem, the old man reflects on the difference between the present and the past, the "laang-time, when yu was me midnight bride,/ Bright, fresh, hopeful, and me lay yu dung dunlopilla bed –/ Downstairs dem a beat drum dem a sing love saang dem a dance in de firelight! . . ./ An me saary bad!" [*Slave Song*, p.36]. As Dabydeen points out in his introduction to *Slave Song* [p.15.] such "brief moments of tenderness, usually in sexual courtship or old age, appear all the more profound and memorable because of the norm of pain". The brutality and violence of the slave's everyday life, and the harsh realities of hunger, exhaustion and pain are reflected in many of the poems, by the poet's use of abrupt, contracted creole forms and images of violation, degradation and brokenness. The use of creole in this way renders the physicality or immediacy of a moment with particular intensity (an effect created by predominantly present tense and imperative formulations in the collection), but it also "speaks the dislocations and oppressions of its history"[25] as a linguistic form. However, the lyrical use of creole is not restricted to the expression of loss, regret or pain; it is also central to those poems, or parts of poems, in which the slave is seen to yearn for transfiguration, imagining his or her release from bound existence through death (as at the end of 'Song of the Creole Gang Women'), or through individual or collective sexual fantasy (as in 'Love Song' and 'The Canecutter's Song'). In such cases the long vowel sounds of creole ("straang", "laang", "haan") and soft endings of words such as "deh", "wheh" and "leh" are emphasized, or a gently flowing alliterative effect ("Leh we go sit dung riverside, dip, dodo, die –/ Shade deep in cool deh" [*Slave Song*, pp. 17-18.]) is employed to contrast with the harsh, staccato effect of the preceding creole.

The editors of *Voiceprint* devote a whole section to elegy and lament, pointing out that "the elegy has become a predominant mode in West Indian poetry"[26]. However, relatively few of the poems they include are in a creole idiom, one notable exception being Linton Kwesi Johnson's 'Reggae for Radni'. David Dabydeen's 'Elegy' in *Slave Song* is both an individual's lament for the loss of his youth, his male companions, his woman and a "lament for the incipient passing" [*Slave Song*, p.59] of a whole way of life in rural Guyana; it can be read as the "depiction of a truncated world that turns in upon itself and questions itself"[27]. As is the case with 'Men and Women', much of the pathos of the poem derives from the fact of old age, exacerbated in this poem by the dreaming confusion and incomprehension of change on the part of the old man: "An is wha mek?" [*Slave Song*, p.36]. In such a context, the familiar names and creole idiom of the poem signify one important continuity in the old man's life amidst so many discontinuities; such unconscious linguistic resistance to the Walcottian edict, "To change your language you must change your life" has rarely been so painfully dramatized.

It is important that we do not assume Dabydeen's adaptation of Guyanese creole to be a naturalistic, or even necessarily a representative one. The literary reconstruction of this medium of vocalization is necessarily a contrivance, an artifice, a self-conscious process. Even writers such as Selvon, whose fictional use of creole was considered naturalistic by many of his earliest (British) critics, has openly acknowledged the need to "modify the dialect"[28]; the creative use of the raw materials of Caribbean speech involves, for him at least, a carefully constructed adaptation, even simulation of the language as *heard*.

Dabydeen's use of creole in *Slave Song* may be a political choice but it is also highly artful. The poet accords his creole-speaking poetic personae an autonomy of voice, a subject position within a discourse which was historically denied their real-life counterparts. Intense individual experience thus becomes the platform from which Dabydeen launches his powerful examination of what (fellow Guyanese writer) Wilson Harris has termed the "pornography of Empire", his exploration of the various means of self-expressive resistance open to the slave – linguistic, gestural and sexual. In his introduction to the collection, Dabydeen speaks of a "crisscross of illusions" [*Slave Song*, p.9] between England and Guiana, mythically figured as 'El Dorado'; this notion of illusion as public mythology is neatly mirrored by Dabydeen's admission that the poems are, in part, "an imaginative rendition ... a private fantasy" [*Slave Song*, p.10]. Indeed, illusion and fantasy run through the collection as organising motifs, but the ultimate irony is that the 'autonomy' of Dabydeen's creole-speaking personae and his poetic use of creole itself are also illusory, fantastical. They are contained, challenged, even silenced, by the translations and notes in Standard English provided by Dabydeen at the end of the collection.

Such Standard English translations might be seen as the ironic legacy of a whole colonial history of indigenous voices being represented, mediated through the colonizer and attenuated or obfuscated in the process. Dabydeen has spoken of the Standard English speaker's use of creole as necessitating a painful "unsheathing of the tongue" in preparation for a "language uncomfortably raw" [*Slave Song*, p.14], yet paradoxically the energy and radicalism of the poems themselves, powerfully disruptive of linguistic hegemonies and canonical modes, is smothered, resheathed and "made tame" by the Standard English translations and the Eurocentric critical apparatus which encases them. It is as if "the reader's need to consult the scholarly appendages to the poems was essentially in order to distance and detoxify the emotional effects of their message"[29]. The notes and translations are, in their own way, as insistent as the creole voices of *Slave Song;* as competing voices they act as a kind of metacommentary on the continuing problematic relationship between First and Third World Literatures, the "crisscross of illusions" and the relationship of inequality which shadows all interpretative acts in this arena. Mark McWatt makes a similar point when he observes how *Slave Song's* promotion/incorporation of its own critical apparatus effectively anticipates the hermeneutic requirements of a metropolitan audience (as the images of the conspicuous consumption of 'peasant' literature by Oxbridge diners at the end of 'Coolie Odyssey' will make even more overt): *"Slave Song* [draws] attention to interesting problems of poetic form and voice, of the ways in which the projected audience of the poem modified the craft itself, so that the poet of ex-colonial societies bears the multiple burden of messenger, translator, apologist, explicator"[30]. However, it could be argued that the notes and translations are deliberately included as an integral part of the text rather than a subtext incorporated under any such 'burden' or obligation; Dabydeen assumes different roles and modes of discourse – historian, polemicist, poet and critic among them, not through necessity but deliberately, in order to subvert conventional generic boundaries and to problematize definitions of social documentation and imaginative reconstruction, primary text and secondary text, testimony and artifact in relation to *Slave Song*.

McWatt also argues that Dabydeen "emphasizes his separation from the lives of the singers by adopting the pose of scholar and translator"[31]. Again, I would argue that this appropriation of the 'authoritative' voice of the metropolitan critic is more subversive; not only does it allow Dabydeen to speak tellingly of the double words and worlds he inhabits as Indo-Caribbean writer and (Black) British critic/academic but it also effectively breaks down the dualities between centre and periphery, critic and writer, literate and illiterate, literary and non-literary, standard and creole by showing that the authority of the critic is illusory, provisional and moreover, one which is readily mimicked – mimicry as "spectacular resistance" being one of the characteristics of postcolonial discourse, as defined by Homi Bhabha[31]. Dabydeen inhabits all these modes in *Slave Song* and the Dabydeen of the notes and translations to *Slave Song* is merely assuming the last in a series of masks in the collection – there are no originary voices in *Slave Song*, only reconstructed, represented, mediating ones.

If Dabydeen genuinely wished to make a significant contribution to the "very little Creole poetry" [*Slave Song*, p.15.] which he perceived as existing at the time of writing *Slave Song*, why did he then include over 27 pages of notes and Standard English translations – more in total than the 25 pages of the actual texts of the poems? It is in the notes and translations, more than anywhere else in the collection, that the real artfulness of *Slave Song* is evidenced: a postmodernist concern with parody and playfulness which flirts with the experiments of modernism, mediating constantly between the particularities of a creole/creolized Guyanese experience and the universalizing orthodoxies of much Western literary criticism. In this respect, Dabydeen's experiments in brokenness might be seen to refer to more linguistic experimentation and to include experimentation with form and genre, for *Slave Song* as a whole raises the question "where do we draw the dividing line between writer and critic, poetry and its interpretation, elucidation and obfuscation?".

Slave Song is a text – like Eliot's *The Waste Land* before it and Brathwaite's *X-Self* after it – which moves towards self-reflexive interpretation and which inscribes its own, wider, problematic positioning within conflicting discourses, different linguistic, literary and cultural legacies. Brathwaite's inclusion of extensive notes to *X-Self* opens up similar 'problems' to those generated by T.S. Eliot's notes to *The Waste Land*. It has been argued that Eliot's notes, whilst appearing to explicate the genesis and complex intertextuality of *The Waste Land*, are in fact an extension of the text deliberately designed to foster its obscurity and its deferral of certainties through the splintering not only of consciousness, but also of language, time and memory. In short, Eliot's notes act as a kind of metacommentary on the *mechanics* of elucidation whilst raising more questions in relation to the poem than they in fact answer. The initial effect of the Notes, as in *Slave Song,* is to underprivilege the internal logic of the poem's own syncretic movement toward greater understanding and to foreground instead the externalised, reductive scrabbling for significance which characterizes so much Western critical practice. The tantalizing suggestion that the notes provide the keys or interpretative codes to unlock the text is little short of a tease; rather than providing closure, they displace our search for authoritative source materials and mythic ur-narratives into an inward and increasingly futile spiral of self-referentiality; if the notes reveal nothing else, they reveal the strength of our hermeneutic desires and the ease with which they can be mocked, and be manipulated, by a wily combination of mimetic and critical functions on the poet's part.

The ambiguous and ultimately subversive function of Eliot's Notes to *The Waste Land* has not been without its imitators. *The Waste Land* to a degree generates its own system of logic and this can be seen as characteristically Modernist. The endless cycle to find meaning in a meaningless world, to know anything with certainty ("What shall we do tomorrow/ What shall we ever do?"), to "only connect" in Forster's words rather than merely "shor[ing] up fragments against [the] ruins", a "heap of broken images" at that – this is not only the moving force of this particular poem but also the quintessential modernist dilemma. Brathwaite's genius in his long poem, *X-Self,* is to reduce the modernist experimentation in brokenness to the level of aesthetic dalliance, by inscribing on this palimpsest the much more powerful trope of fragmentation as historical experience, paradigmatic of the African diasporic experience – and of the Caribbean condition more generally[32].

The relationship between Eliot's and Brathwaite's poetry has been well documented[33]; what is less often noted is that in *X-Self,* his most densely allusive poem to date, Brathwaite reveals an

awareness that his poetry might be criticized for an 'obscurity'
similar to that levelled at Eliot's *The Waste Land*. Brathwaite ex-
plains in his notes to *X-Self* that because his poems are based on
a culture that is both "personal" and "multifarious": "My references may appear mysterious, meaningless even, to both Caribbean and non-Caribbean readers"[34]. Again, the projected
(eurocentric) audience plays a crucial role in the shaping of this
poetic work. Brathwaite openly admits that he provides the notes:

> With great reluctance, since the irony is that they may sug-
> gest the poetry is so obscure in itself that it has to be lighted
> up; [that] it is so lame, that it has to have a crutch; and
> (most hurtful of all) [a concern intimately related to Brath-
> waite's central interest in the patterns of music, song and
> orality and a fear of their negation] that it is bookish, aca-
> demic, 'history'.

The same kind of tension between the desire to make use of
those essentially oral features of his linguistic and cultural heritage – "dub riddums and nation language and calibanisms" and
the contrary appearance given by the notes, of them "coming from
a learned (and significantly *written*) treatise" – is explored in
Slave Song but to a different end. Brathwaite envisages his poem
as the positive realisation of a "magical realism" of improvisations in a "quicksilver" language of boundless imaginative possibilities but is simultaneously aware of the danger of this being
buried under the dominant impression of a reliance on predeter-
mined textual fragments; he fears that these fragments will turn
out to be overwhelmingly non-Caribbean in origin, culturally and
linguistically alien to the Caribbean realities he is trying to explore and address. Traces of Foucault's metaphor of the archaeo-
logical dig surface in Brathwaite's clarification of his point:

> The impression [will be], in other words, that I write the
> poems from the notes, when in fact I have to dig up these

notes from fragments, glimpses, partial memories (it would take a lifetime to track them down), and the only satisfaction I get is the fascination of watching the counterpoint emerge of 'fact versus the fiction' of the poetry... in many cases, like you, I am reading these notes for the first time.

One senses something of the same experimental quality in the notes (without the same degree of artistic anxiety) in Dabydeen's *Slave Song*, published some three years earlier. *Slave Song's* notes are altogether less transparent, more artful. That a playful relationship between poems and the notes/translations was evidently intended is made clear by Dabydeen's comment: "People like Brathwaite have been arguing for years that Creole is a different language, sufficiently different from English to be considered its own language. So therefore the logic would be to provide a translation, which is what I did"[35]. The whole critical apparatus of *Slave Song* ostensibly exists to comment on the main body of the poems but as in Argentinian Manuel Puig's postmodernist novel, *Kiss of the Spider-Woman*, the critical apparatus gradually takes over the text, asserting its own autonomy by (literally) appropriating textual space, blurring the boundaries between creative and critical discourse, text and subtext, empiricism and a creatively reconstructed theoretical discourse.

If we take Dabydeen's comments to their logical conclusion it is possible to arrive at a very different reading of *Slave Song*, one which sees the introduction, notes and translations as self-aggrandizing texts which claim their own 'autonomy', asserting their dominance by adopting a separate – and privileged – language. The distinction between subverting the linguistic hegemonies and canonical modes of the centre and reproducing them is often a very fine one, and in *Slave Song*, it is possible to see the standard English voices asserting a reconstituted cultural supremacy, slipping into the easy grooves of long-established literary and linguistic hegemonies, falling back on the Western privileging of

standardized forms over dialectal ones, the privileging of interpretative over primary materials.

Wilson Harris has termed the introduction and notes to *Slave
Song* "useful, indeed essential" and the translations "a necessary
ingredient of the book . . . strengthening one's appreciation of a
kind of internal sculpture in the poem that may be minted from
altered vowel and consonant sounds in [creole]"[36]. The prose
notes to *Slave Song* may enrich the poems' meanings, but the
translations of the poems into standard English tend to have the
opposite effect. Dabydeen himself acknowledges that such translation attenuates the creole language which is not merely the ve-
hicle, but indeed the substance of thought. Alongside this is lost
the "Creole choreography" [*Slave Song*, p. 65.] of the rhythms of
song, work and life; a whole world of gesture and kinetic energy
contained in the language is at once made "lame". A similar pull
between enrichment and impoverishment of understanding, between explication and obfuscation which characterized Eliot's
notes, can thus be seen to be enacted in *Slave Song*.

An alternative is to read the notes/ translations as a deliberate
and organic part of the collection. The mediating voices of white
amanuenses, who introduced (socially and textually) the
published narratives and oral testimonies of slaves and ex-slaves
in the last two centuries, especially in North America, are
replaced in *Slave Song*, by a self-generated critical introduction
which parodically 'authorizes' the text for white or non-creole-
speaking consumption. Superficially, the notes/translations
gesture towards the interpretative possibilities of the poems whilst
in fact circumscribing the range of meanings; on a deeper level,
they engage with more fundamental critical issues such as the
problematic 'consumption' and reception of the postcolonial text
in Europe, the need to decentre outmoded binaries and to re-
appropriate the role of critic, self-reflexively. The critical
apparatus of *Slave Song* also enacts the radical subversion of
generic categories by skilfully inhabiting and impersonating

multiple modes of discourse (literary and sociological analysis, polemic translation). Arguably, the fluency and continuities of the notes, the 'access' to the poems which they apparently facilitate, is only superficial; their hybridized 'authority', the radical disjunction of their linguistic power base and milieu from the creole experience which the poems inscribe, encourages an awareness of brokenness operating as an aesthetic of deliberate unevenness, disturbance or interruption in the collection as a whole. *Slave Song*, viewed in this light, is a text playfully self-conscious of the illusory or provisional nature of its own autonomies and of textual 'authority' generally (as is enacted in the reconstitution of dominant voices in the Notes); its different voices (creole, standard, slave, poet, critic) reveal the paradoxical nature of power and subjectivity to be never truly autonomous, always determined. Moreover, *Slave Song* inscribes its own subversion only to reinscribe the old hegemonies; for example, the collection is characterized by a vigorous orality but also a deeply interiorized – and ultimately stronger – textuality; like the published text of *Lionheart Gal*[37], it is a radical experimental text of mediated voices which "somewhat ironically affirms the authority of the written word"[38]. The "new indenture"[39] for the postcolonial writer, as Mark McWatt suggests, may well be no less than "literature" itself.

Notes

1   Mrs Carmichael, *Domestic Manners and Social Condition of the White, Coloured and Negro Population of the West Indies*, 2 vols. (New York: Negro Universities Press, 1969; originally published London: Whittaker, Treacher & Co., 1833), i, p.5.

2   Robert Southey, 'The New Testament in the Negro Tongue', *New Quarterly Review*, 43 (October 1830), pp. 553-564 (p.564).

3   *The Trinidad Review*, Port of Spain, June 19, 1869.

4   Introduction to *Slave Song* (Aarhus: Dangaroo Press: 1984), p.13.

5   Edward Long, absentee planter from Jamaica wrote *A History of Jamaica*, the classic text of the apologist tradition, after a 12 year residence in the

island; it was originally published in London in 1774 and was repub-
lished by Frank Cass in 1970.

6   James Anthony Froude, Emeritus Professor of History at Oxford Univer-
     sity, wrote an account of his travels in the West Indies which was pub-
     lished as *The English in the West Indies or the Bow of Ulysses*, in London
     by Longmans, Green & Co. in 1888. Like Long's *History* before it, this
     polemical work carried both intellectual kudos and a certain popular ap-
     peal back in Britain and was profoundly influential in promoting ill-in-
     formed, stereotypical perceptions of the languages and societies of the
     West Indies.

7   These include John Amphlett's *Under a Tropical Sky: a journal of first
     impressions of the West Indies* (London, Sampson Low, Marston Low and
     Searle: 1873) and Joseph Sturge and Thomas Harvey's *The West Indies in
     1837* (London: Macmillan, Adams: 1888; republished in London by
     Dawsons of Pall Mall in 1968).

8   For example, numerous literary reviews of West Indian writers published
     in Britain in the late 1940s, and 1960s replicate the same misapprehen-
     sions and inaccuracies which are wilfully or unintentionally inscribed in
     early European accounts of Caribbean creoles.

9   Such negative images of creole amongst West Indian speakers were due to
     the complex proscriptive legacies of the colonial educational system as
     well as certain other sociolinguistic factors which privilege more stand-
     ardized forms as the means to greater social mobility and social and pro-
     fessional advancement.

10   See for example, John Rickford's analysis of short creole narratives in
     *Dimensions of a Creole Continuum – History, Texts and Linguistic Analysis
     of Guyanese Creole* (Stanford, California, Stanford University Press:
     1987) and Brathwaite's seminal lecture: *The History of the Voice* (London,
     New Beacon: 1984).

11   David Dabydeen spoke in an interview of this "resourcefulness [of creole]
     in conveying certain experiences . . . In the brokenness of the language
     resides not just a certain barbaric energy, but also the capacity to be ex-
     perimental with a language; it is almost like Shakespearean English. You
     can make up words, play with words, and you can rhyme in much more
     adventurous ways than you can in Standard English. The brokenness has
     a capacity to convey a greater sense of tragedy and pain, of energy, but
     you can also reconstruct it in your own way, you can play with the lan-
     guage with a greater degree of freedom" [Interview by Wolfgang Binder,
     Journal of West Indian Literature, 3/2 (Sept. 1989), p. 76].

12   See for example, Linton Kwesi Johnson's *Dread Beat and Blood* (London:
     Race Today: 1975), *Inglan is a Bitch* (London: Race Today: 1980),

Valerie Bloom's *Touch mi! Tell mi!* (London: Bogle l'Ouverture: 1981), James Berry's, *Lucy's Letters and Loving* (London: New Beacon: 1982), Fred D'Aguiar's *Mama Dot* (London: Chatto: 1985), John Agard's *Mangoes and Bullets* (London: Pluto: 1985), Michael Smith's *It a Come* (London: Race Today: 1986), Marc Matthews', *Guyana My Altar* (London: Karnak: 1987), Jean Binta Breeze's *Riddym Ravings and other Poems* (London: Race Today: 1988), Benjamin Zephaniah's *The Dread Affair* (London: Arena: 1985).

13   Paula Burnett, Introduction to *The Penguin Book of Caribbean Verse* (Middlesex: Penguin: 1986), p.xxix.

14   David Dabydeen interviewed by Wolfgang Binder, *Journal of West Indian Literature* 3/2 (Sept. 1989), p. 75.

15   In conversation, October 1990.

16   In *The Star-Apple Kingdom* (London: 1979), pp. 33-35.

17   Benita Parry, "Between Creole and Cambridge English: The Poetry of David Dabydeen", *Kunapipi* X/3 (1988), pp. 1-17. Reproduced in this volume.

18   Benita Parry reads these poems as the chartings of the "sexual pathology" which resulted from the "internalisation of colonialism's institutional and psychological violence" in both slave and slaveholder; however, that the slave's resistance takes the form of "abusing and mutilating the white women [also] implicates the poems in a discourse shared by the master's culture and beyond, one that represents rape as what woman wants" [Parry, op.cit, pp. 5-6].

19   'On Not Being Milton: Nigger Talk in England Today', *Tibisisi*, ed. Maggie Butcher (Dangaroo: 1989), p.121.

20   Binder op. cit., p.75.

21   Benita Parry, for example, recognizes that part of the "ambition" behind the collection is "to articulate in the local idiom the perceptions and dreams of the historically muted, that is, to express what they themselves cannot verbalize because of their lack of words" (Notes, p. 53) [Parry, op. cit., p. 2-3]. This, she argues, amounts to "speaking for others" and "speaking for others is [always] a fiction". To "reinvent the speech and reconceive the fantasies of slaves and peasant canecutters" [ibid, p. 3] may illuminate the historical actuality of slavery but can only do so imaginatively.

22   Dabydeen has spoken of creole as a medium incapable of abstraction, in which "ideas always have to be conveyed sensuously", Binder op. cit., p. 74.

23   In *Hinterland*, edited by E.A.Markham (Newcastle-upon-Tyne: Bloodaxe:1989), pp. 181-182.

24   Ibid, p. 180.

25   Parry op. cit., p.1.

26   *An Anthology of Oral and Related Poetry from the Caribbean*, edited by Stewart Brown, Mervyn Morris and Gordon Rohlehr (Harlow, Essex: Longmans: 1989), p. 17.

27   Wilson Harris, Review of *Slave Song, Kunapipi* (1984).

28   In 'Sam Selvon Talking – A conversation with Kenneth Ramchand', *Canadian Literature*, 95 (Winter 1982), p. 60.

29   Mark McWatt, Review of *Coolie Odyssey, Journal of West Indian Literature*, (Sept. 1989), pp. 86-90.

30   Ibid, p. 87.

31   "Mimicry [is] a form of civil disobedience within the discipline of civility... [a] sign of spectacular resistance", Homi Bhabha, 'Signs Taken for Words', *Critical Inquiry*, 12/1 (Autumn 1985), p. 162.

32   Derek Walcott's delineation of the figurative dimensions of brokenness as geographical pattern, historical paradigm and poetic trope, in his recent Nobel Lecture echoes the archeological metaphors of Brathwaite's Notes to *X-Self*, but takes a more traditional line in foregrounding not an experience of radical fragmentation, but instead the role of the artist in 'reassembling', 'restoring', 'reconstituting' these fragments into a hypothetical 'wholeness' which bears the traces of an inherent brokenness: "Break a vase, and the love that reassembles the fragments is stronger than the love which took its symmetry for granted when it was whole. The glue that fits the pieces is the sealing of its original shape. It is such a love that reassembles our African and Asiatic fragments, the cracked heirlooms whose restoration shows its white scars. This gathering of broken pieces is the care and pain of the Antilles, and if the pieces are disparate, ill-fitting, they contain more pain than their original sculpture, those icons and sacred vessels taken for granted in their ancestral places. Antillean art is the restoration of our shattered histories, our shards of vocabulary, our archipelago becoming a synonym for pieces broken off from the original continent ... and this is the exact process of the making of poetry, or what should be called not its 'making' but its remaking, the fragmented memory ...", 'The Antilles – Fragments of Epic Memory', The Nobel Lecture 1992 (London: Faber and Faber: 1993), p. 9.

33   See, for example, Gordon Rohlehr's self-published, *Pathfinder: Black Awakening in The Arrivants of Edward Kamau Brathwaite* (Tunapuna, Trinidad: 1981).

34   *X-Self* (Oxford: Oxford University Press: 1987) p.113.

35   Binder, op. cit., p.75.

36   Harris, op. cit.

37   Sistren with Honor Ford Smith, editor, *Lionheart Gal: Life Stories of Jamaican Women* (London: The Women's Press, 1986).

38   Carolyn Cooper, 'Writing Oral History: Sistren Theatre Collective's *Lionheart Gal*', Stephen Slemon and Helen Tiffin eds. *After Europe* (Coventry: Dangaroo Press: 1989), p. 51.

39   McWatt, op. cit., p. 88.

CHAPTER III

BETWEEN CREOLE AND CAMBRIDGE
ENGLISH: THE POETRY OF DAVID DABYDEEN

BENITA PARRY
(I)

David Dabydeen's poetry belongs with "a literature in broken English".[1] In this revised usage, the odium directed at deviations from an ethnocentrically prescribed form is displaced by the recognition that the writing practices of those who are outside the dominant culture have opened 'Eng. Lit.' to heterogeneous and heretical modes. The notion has been differently deployed by Dabydeen to define the Creole of his native Guyana as a hybrid language which speaks the dislocations and oppressions of its history:

> A feature of the language is its brokenness, no doubt reflecting the brokenness and suffering of its original users — African slaves and East Indian indentured labourers. Its potential as a naturally tragic language is there, there in its brokenness and rawness which is like the rawness of a wound. (Introduction to *Slave Song*, pp. 13-14)

The power of language as a means of subjugation, and conversely as the affirmation of values, perspectives and traditions despised or disregarded by colonial discourses, is a concept central to critiques of 'Third World' texts and the 'minority' writings of internally exiled communities such as Afro-Americans, Chicanos, Aborigines, Maoris and British Blacks. One position, represented by Ngugi wa Thiong'o, insists that since language is "the collective memory bank of a people's experience in history", the postcolonial world can only repossess the signifying function usurped by imperialism through the use of native languages.[2] Other critics, extending a proposition of Deleuze and Guattari,[3] argue that the heterodox practices of the culturally exiled who write in a 'major' language produce a counter-discourse articulating another consciousness and sensibility in the process of decodifying or 'deterritorializing' the forms and categories of 'great literature'. Whether written in the native languages or in those of the imperialist nations, a polyglot postcolonial literature, disruptive of canonical modes, enters the lists as a refusal of the cultural supremacy still exercised by the metropolitan centres. At stake is the self-definition of radical cultural difference in its multiple registers, a practice which positions the colonial and postcolonial worlds as subject, wrenching from the West the power of producing the other hemisphere as the deviant form of its Self. "To represent the colonial subject is to conceive the subject of difference, of an-other history and an-other culture".[4] Such writing will resist assimilation by a literary criticism whose insistent rhetoric of universals effaces both the historical conditions within which texts are produced and the specificities they speak. What is instead required of critiques is attention to the breaking of rules and the dismantling of authorized structures:

> Many arguments can be made for the importance and interest of non-canonical forms of literature such as that of the third world, but one is peculiarly self-defeating because it borrows the weapons of the adversary: the strategy of trying to prove that these texts are as 'great' as those of the canon itself.[5]

As critic, Dabydeen has contributed to the projects of restoring to visibility the black presence in English writing and art that has

been marginalized in analytical discussion.[6] As poet he is an eloquent black presence. In an essay, 'On Not Being Milton: Nigger
Talk in England Today', he places his poetry within those noncon-
formist traditions where established structures are disrupted and
'standard' English deliberately 'misused' by those to whom the
language is both an imperialist legacy and a step-mother-tongue:

> I cannot . . . feel or write poetry like a white man, much less
> serve him . . . I feel that I am different, not wholly, but suffi-
> cient for me to want to contemplate that which is other in
> me, which owes its life to particular rituals of ancestry.[7]

In search of a language that will speak the Guyanese history
and landscape, Dabydeen has written in Creole and in English
which, as Henry Louis Gates has said of all black texts written in
a western language, is "two-toned . . . Its visual tones are white
and black, and its aural tones are standard and vernacular".[8] The
many linguistic registers of his poetry enunciate a self dispersed
between affiliation to Indian parentage, solidarity with Guyana's
history of conquest, colonization and slavery, and a consciousness
irreversibly marked and fissured by English education and residence, the disparate facets held together within a black identity.
His is diaspora as a permanent condition while remaining bound
to a natal culture he can no longer inhabit; and his verse, which
is part of the process in Caribbean writing of opening up the African, Indian and Amerindian experiences, can be read as a debt to
the ancestors.

The ambition of *Slave Song* is to articulate in the local idiom
the perceptions and dreams of the historically muted, that is, to
express what "they themselves cannot verbalize because of their
lack of words" ("Notes," p. 53). But 'speaking for' others is a fiction, and although it is Dabydeen's stated intention to 'describe'
ways of being and seeing based on "a jumble of fact and myth,
past and present", ("Introduction," p.10) what he does is reinvent

the speech and reconceive the fantasies of slaves and peasant canecutters – and often in verse forms that can owe as much to manipulating or parodying English modes as to oral tradition. 'Guyana Pastoral', for instance, a lament for the rape and murder of an Indian girl, undermines the sanitized rendering of Caribbean plantation life in eighteenth century English verse and the slavish imitation of this style in what Dabydeen calls the tourist doggerel of early Guyanese versifiers. The harshly accented metre violates pastoral poesy; the convention of moon, sun and wind as benign images in this convention is subverted by recitation of their absence, and another order of naming indigenous to the Guyanese landscape erases the mystique of nature's sublimity:

> Under de tambrin tree whe de moon na glow
> Laang, laang, laang, she lay, laang, laang
> She cry, but de wind na blow
> An dem wraang an straang
> An dem wuk an dem bruk till fowlcack-crow.
> Who see who hear when she belly buss, when she mout splash blood?
> Only de jumbie umbrella dat poke up e white eye from de mud.

In this collection are celebrations of food rituals ('For Ma'), the rendering of peasant wit pitted against the 'English' pretensions of an upwardly mobile youth, ('Two Cultures'), and an elegy to the failure of domestic relations ('Men and Women'). The central preoccupation, however, is with protesting a history of untold oppressions and a present of relentless exploitation in a language that is "angry, crude, energetic". The cutlass, sickle and blade that hack, cut, chop and stab at the cane invoke the punishing labour of working on sugar plantations; chain, lash and whip image the condition and memories of slavery; piranha, snake and alligator are figures in an inhospitable landscape. Together these tropes overturn the vision of Arcadia delivered to the West by Raleigh's *The Discovery of the Large, Rich and Beautiful Empire of Guiana* and perpetuated in subsequent English literature. The voice in *Slave Song* is overwhelmingly that of public protestation. In 'Slavewoman's Song', the inferred exchanges between a speaker and an addressee imply a lament for shared sorrows:

> Ya howl –
> Hear how ya howl –
> Tell me wha ya howl foh
> Tell me noh?
> Pickni?
> Dem tek pickni way?
> Wha dem do wid pickni
> Mek yu knaack yu head wid stone
> Bite yu haan like daag-bone?

while 'Song of the Creole Gang Women' reworks a communal work song in the interlocution of women's voices execrating the usurpation and abuse of their bodies:

> Wuk, nuttin bu wuk
> Maan noon an night nuttin bu wuk
> Booker own me patacake
> Booker own me pickni.
> Pain, nuttin bu pain
> Waan million tous'ne acre cane.
> O since me baan – juk! juk! juk! juk! juk!
> So sun in me eye like taan
> So Booker saach deep in me flesh
> Kase Booker own me rass
> An Booker own me cutlass –

(II)

The physicality of the language which is the poetry's strength also signals its danger. Of *Slave Song* Dabydeen has written that he set out to deal with the Romance of Cane, "meaning the perverse eroticism of black labour and the fantasy of domination, bondage and sadomasochism . . . The subject demanded a language capable of describing both a lyrical and a corrosive sexuality" ('On Not Being Milton'). A project exposing the "pornography of empire" may well itself need to utter obscenities in mapping the convergence of sexuality with the lived experience of an oppression that is racial and economic. When such writing simultaneously articulates and interrogates the heightened and morbid erotic energies released by colonialism, it will generate its own critique. This is the case with the polyphonic *Coolie Odyssey*, as it is with the requiem for the rape of Indian girls in *Slave Song*, which laments the deeds of men whose "savage imagination is the correlate to the physical savagery of their work" ("Notes," p. 53). However, in that disturbing set of poems, which condense the internalization of colonialism's institutional and psychological violence, there is no dialogue with the direct represented discourse of speakers whose sexuality has been channelled into the desire to inflict and receive pain, and with whose imaginative transition from Romance to rape, the reader is invited to identify.

That colonialism engendered a sexual pathology in both black and white, women and men, is not in question. What is at issue is how texts speak these psychoses. The slave, who proudly resists the master's degradations by asserting an uncolonized sexuality, dreams of taking revenge by abusing the slave owner's wife:

> Whip me till me bleed
> Till me beg.
> Tell me how me hanimal
> African orang-utan
> Tell me how me cannibal

Fit fo slata fit fo hang.

. . .

Bu yu caan stap me cack dippin in de honeypot
Dripping at de tip an happy as a hottentot!

. . .

If so when yu dun dream she pink tit,
Totempole she puss,
Leff yu teetmark like tattoo in she troat!
('Slave Song', pp. 28 and 30)

The canecutters, who perceive in the white woman the image of
their search for better things, are overtaken by the desire to defile
and maim her, an assault which the speakers see her as inviting:

White hooman walk tru de field fo watch we canecutta,
Tall, straight, straang-limb,

. . .

Wash dis dutty-skin in yu dew
Wipe am clean on yu saaf white petal!
O Shanti! Shanti! Shanti!
So me spirit call, so e halla foh yu

. . .

But when night come how me dream . . .
Dat yu womb lie like starapple buss open in de mud
And how me hold yu dung, wine up yu waiss
Draw blood from yu patacake, daub am all over yu face
Till yu dutty like me and yu halla
Like when cutlass slip an slice me leg . . .
('The Canecutters' Song', pp. 25, 26)

A canecutter who declaims *his* febrile version of a white woman's nightmare, attributes to *her* a lust for violation:

Bruk dung de door!
Waan gang sweat-stink nigga

Drag she aff she bed
Wuk pun she
Crack she head
Gi she jigga
Tween she leg!
. . .
Wet she awake cuss de daybreak!
('Nightmare', p. 34)

The frenzied imagination spoken by male black voices is balanced by the cries of black women for sexual gratification, even at the hands of the master whose exploitation causes their bodies' agony:

Everything tie up, haat, lung, liver, an who go loose me caad?
Shaap, straight, sudden like pimpla, cut free
An belly buss out like blood-flow a shriek?
Or who saaf haan, saaf-flesh finga?
Or who go paste e mout on me wound, lick, heal, like starapple suck?
('Song of the Creole Gang Women', p. 18)

The field which an oppositional writing contests is densely mined by colonialist representation. As Fanon has written, for the white person, the black is the biological, the genital, the sexual instinct in its raw state, she is concupiscence, sexual prowess and performance.[9] And in these poems, I would argue, pain, frustration and anger is spoken by the native positioned as the very figure of phobic white fears and desires – even though such paranoia is derided, even though the sadism/masochism is invoked as a disorientated spiritual aspiration. Moreover, what is troubling to this reader is that as the cut, chop, hack and stab of "the savage ceremony of cane" takes possession of the imagination of male canecutter and slave, the rage against their condition is spent in fantasies of abusing and mutilating the white woman. Dabydeen deliberately and provocatively implicates the poems in a discourse shared by the master's culture and beyond, one that represents rape as what woman wants.[10] It could be anticipated that a poetry refusing colonialism's misconstructions would displace its premises. When Fanon analysed how the native under colonial conditions assimilates as self-knowledge and acts out in conduct those features ascribed to him or her by the master, he acknowledges his own capitulation to the white person's denigratory gaze:

> The black man has no ontological resistance in the eyes of the white man . . . I was responsible at the same time for my body, for my race, for my ancestors. I subjected myself to an objective examination, I discovered my blackness, my ethnic characteristics; and I was battered down by tom-toms, cannibalism, intellectual deficiency, fetishism, racial defects, slave ships. (*Black Skin, White Masks*, p. 112).

It is against such surrender that Fanon's writing intercedes to construct an alternative mode of self-presentation. If the reading I have proposed is valid (it is one that may, and I hope will, be contested), can the same be said of these particular poems in *Slave Song*?

(III)

Where *Slave Song* offers a fiction of transparency, of instant access to the authentically demotic voices of Guyana, *Coolie Odyssey* satirizes the conceit of poets aspiring to retrieve a folk heritage:

> Now that peasantry is in vogue,
> Poetry bubbles from peat bogs,
> People strain for the old folk's fatal gobs
> Coughed up in grates North or North East

'Tween bouts o' living dialect
('Coolie Odyssey', p.9)

The illusion that the poet is transmitting the consciousness and
unconscious of others sustained in *Slave Song* is dispelled in this
collection by the presence of the poet as speaking subject. Here it
is his address which appropriates the topos of the epic voyage to
tell the story of the multiple dislocations in a Caribbean history:

It should be time to hymn your own wreck,
Your house the source of ancient song
('Coolie Odyssey', p. 9)

Hence the title is without any connotation of oxymoron, signalling as it does a project celebrating the unsung heroic journeys
made across geographical space, between languages, from a peasant to a late capitalist mode of production; a journey where Home
is never a place of rest, but always the name of what has been ir-
retrievably lost, to be regained only in verse. The passage is from
India to Guyana, where Old Dabydeen always dreaming of India,

Washed obsessively by the canal bank,
Spread flowers on the snake-infested water,
Fed the gods the food that Chandra cooked,
Bathed his tongue of the creole
Babbled by low-caste infected coolies.
('Coolie Odyssey', p. 10)

Self-exiled from Guyana, "young Dabydeen", "Who move out
from mud and walk England", ('Ma Talking Words', p. 40) commemorates what he had left:

We mark your memory in songs
Fleshed in the emptiness of folk,
Poems that scrape bowl and bone

In English basements far from home
('Coolie Odyssey', p. 13)

Returning to Guyana, the expatriate is appalled by the tourists' perception to which he now has access:

How they clearly passing you like beggarman
But perplexed your blessed sunshine country
Should breed such you-lice, shacks.
('Homecoming', p. 43)

The poetry oscillates between the irony of the attempt to reincarnate in verse an original condition that never was, and the obligation on the poet to write the story of those silenced by history:

I brace you up against a wall
Doom-laden, mugging you for a life-story.
I trade you rum for old-time Indian talk
But you stutter creole stupidness, yielding
No gift but a sackful of green mangoes.
History we greed for in England,
Must know coolie ship, whip, brown paddy-skins
Burst, blown far by winds,
Whilst pearl-white rice feed overseer-mouth:
England, where it snows but we still born brown,
That I come back from to here, home,
As hungry as any white man for native gold,
To plant flag and to map your mind.
('Homecoming', p. 43)

The bitterness of the expatriate writer, who by reiterating the tropes of colonialism's text places himself in the position of the colonizer, is assuaged by the map his verse draws, one on which the configuration of colours conceptualizes an aboriginal perception of social landscape and history.

There is ambivalence too in the poet who, on returning to "this library of graves" for a funeral, acknowledges the claim on him of forebears who discounted themselves and whose lives went unremarked and unhonoured:

> There are no headstones, epitaphs, dates.
> The ancestors curl and dry to scrolls of parchment.
> They lie like texts
> Waiting to be written by the children
> For whom they hacked and ploughed and saved
> To send to faraway schools.
> *Is foolishness fill your head.*
> *Me dead.*
> *Dog-bone and dry-well*
> *Got no story to tell.*
> *Just how me born stupid is so me gone.*
> Still we persist before the grave
> Seeking fables.
> We plunder for the maps of El Dorado
> To make bountiful our minds in an England
> Starved of gold.
> ('Coolie Odyssey', p. 12)

The self-conscious poet who privileges writing as constitutive of meaning – the past is a "library of graves", the ancestors are documents written in an antique script – simultaneously performs an act of communication that inserts the writing into a social process. Now, instead of speaking for a community, the poet addresses himself to them, conversing with them in a language that is "two-toned" and producing their story which is also his own history. This act of recollection is not a recall of a pre-existent condition but the conception of writing of what they themselves drafted in their deeds, and which "young Dabydeen" with his access to an English education and print technology will return to them. So fine an ambition does not go unchallenged by the peasant scepticism of "Ma", herself a virtuoso word player, deriding the vanity of poetry:

> That is dream and air!
> You can't make pickni from word
> Howsoever beautiful or raging:
> The world don't know word.
>
> . . .
>
> Book learning you got,
> But history done dead . . .
> ('Ma Talking Words', pp. 40-41)

(IV)

In appropriating and alienating the tropes of colonialism's texts, Dabydeen's poetry produces an intensely focused critique of colonialist appetites and practices. Recurrently, gold is degraded into images of abused labour, as in cane and canefields, or into a figure of violent conquest: "Yellow of the palm of dead Amerindian/Unyielding gold" ('The Old Map', p. 14). In 'El Dorado', the object of desire in the conquistadors' and colonisers' quest after the Amerindian legend is simultaneously debased in sustained metaphors of exploitation, and redeemed through the grace of an oppressed community honouring its "gilded one":

> Juncha slowly dying of jaundice
> Or yellow fever or blight or jumbie or neighbour's spite,
> No-one knows why he turns the colour of cane.
>
> . . .
>
> Skin flaking like goldleaf
> Casts a halo round his bed.
> He goes out in a puff of gold dust.
>
> . . .
>
> They bury him like treasure,
> The coolie who worked two shillings all day
> But kept his value from the overseer. (p.15)

Coolie Odyssey is haunted by a word that came to Europe via Columbus, was later anagrammatically reinscribed in *The Tempest* and perpetuated by *Robinson Crusoe*. Of the power of this word, Peter Hulme has written:

> Discursively the Caribbean is a special place, partly because of its primacy in the encounter between Europe and America, civilization and savagery, and partly because it has been seen as the location, physically and etymologically, of the practice, that more than any other, is the mark of unregenerate savagery – cannibalism. 'Cannibalism' . . . is the special, perhaps even defining, feature of the discourse of colonialism as it pertained to the native Caribbean.[11]

As the poems variously and ingeniously invoke this 'defining feature', detaching it from 'Caribbean savagery', there is a shift in the semantic field. 'Bone' is reiterated as a figure of social deprivation; the baby feeding at a mother's breast "Cannibalize she nipple" ('Christmas in the Caribbean', p. 23); the act of cannibalism is mimicked and metamorphosed in sexual encounters:

> Lapped at her ego
> Like the mouth of beasts
>
> . . .
>
> Sucked her distress
> Like berries from her gaping vein
> ('Water with Berries', p. *36*)
>
> . . .
>
> She wanted to suck words,
> Violate some mystery,
> Feed deep, delirious
> Into some gleaming tropical vein
>
> . . .

> He clamped his loins
> From her consumptive mouth
> ('New World Words', p. 37)

The daemon is briskly demystified by the Englishwoman oppressed by the black man's obsession with the self-image imposed
on him:

> She wanted to be alone with her world, vexed
> Always by his prehistoric eye,
> The strange usurping tales of anthropophagi
> And recitation of colonial texts.
> ('The New Poetry', p. 28)

And it is exorcised by the memory of a joyous crab feast, its
pleasures contrasted with the bleakness of expatriation:

> Tonight we'll have one big happy curry feed,
> We'll test out who teeth and jaw strongest
> Who will grow up to be the biggest
> Or who will make most terrible cannibal.
> We leave behind a mess of bones and shell
> And come to England and America
> Where Ruby hustles in a New York tenement
> And me writing poetry in Cambridge
> ('Catching Crabs', p. 44)

To demythologize 'Caliban' requires yet more complex moves.
At the centre of the collection, both in its ordering and its
engagement with the white world's construction of its others, are
the poems invoking the incommensurable wants it encounters
between black man and white woman who find themselves cast in
the roles of 'Caliban' and 'Miranda' written by colonialism. When
the poet as supplicant black man yearns for the white woman as
lover/mother to heal his psychic pain and redeem his degraded

image, it is Caliban's speech that he borrows for his text – and for
the title of one poem:

> That when he woke he cried to dream again
> Of the scent of her maternity
> ('Miranda', p. 33)
> . . . he, forever imprisoned
> In a romance of history
> Emerges from sleep as from ship's bowel
> Desperate to dream again
> In her white spacious body
> ('Water With Berries', p. 36)

However, both the concupiscent, disobedient Caliban and the
pristine figureheads of the civil society that perpetrated colonialism are parodied in the witty dialogue of 'The Seduction' where
the speakers define themselves negatively in relationship to the
stereotypes – as is poetic form since the sexual tensions complicit
with colonial history are sung in the simple syntax, metre and
rhyming couplets of the ballad:

> She said her name was Kate
> And whether he would mate
> On such and such a date
> Or else tonight before too late
> Before the pause to contemplate
> Before the history and the hate.

>> I cannot come to you tonight
>> With monstrous organ of delight
>> I have no claw no appetite
>> I am not Caliban but sprite
>> But weakness flutterance and flight
>> An insect scurrying from the light.

She said her name was really Jane
That she was sweet as sugarcane
Unblighted by colonial reign
That all he wanted was some pain
To wrap himself in mythic chain
And labour in his self-disdain.

> You know that I am flaccid black
> Yet stretch my skin upon a rack
> That I may reach whereof I lack
> And scrape away the mange and plaque
> Of legacy and looking back
> Obliterate the ancient track

That I am naked lost in shame
Without the fantasy and game
The rules that history did proclaim –
I am the torture: you the flame
I am the victim: you the blame –
Tell me again, what is your name?

> Britannia it is not she cries!
> Miranda also she denies!
> Nor map nor piracy nor prize
> Nor El Dorado in disguise
> With pity gazed into his eyes
> And saw he could not improvise (pp.30, 31)

The disjunctions of this dialogue are implicit in the series of poems about the 'white woman'. The black man's sexuality is imprisoned in a dream world inhabited by images of sun-god, cane and overseer, slave ships and "a cornucopia of slaves poured overboard", by chain, rack and whiplash, by:

The howling oceanic thrust of history
That heaved forth savages in strange canoes
('The Sexual Word', p.32)

The liberation he seeks in her embrace is refused by the white
woman who can respond to his poetry but not to the importunities
of his demand that she enter into his phantasmagoria: "She for-
sook as tedious his confession . . ." ('The New Poetry', p.28);
"She refused the embrace of fantasy . . ." ('The Sexual Word',
p.32). In another incarnation, the white woman expropriates the
black man to serve her desire for the primitive, seeing him as
"Goldleaf or edge of assagai" ('Caliban', p.34), or probing him for
"some gleaming tropical vein" ('New World Words', p.37). In
keeping with an 'Odyssey' that is a journey without arrivals, there
is no repossession of a sexuality whose privacies have been invaded by colonialist representation, only the struggle to confront
and disavow the positions this imposes.

Dabydeen's is a radical poetry, sensuous and political,
nourished by images of the enslaved past endured by generations
of the downtrodden; its atavism is not a retrograde worship of the
ancestors but a rewriting of the West's master narrative that
addresses the postcolonial condition. He writes not only as a
Guyanese within a Caribbean tradition, but as a British Black who
has known the "winter of England's scorn" and whose poetry
defies the racist fear that "They will besmirch the White Page
with their own words". The irony, of which Dabydeen is aware, is
that prominent in his audience are "congregations of the
educated" who are white, and if as Ma maintains "White people
don't want to heal their own scar or hear their own story", then to
whom are the poems addressed? Dabydeen is being ingenuous
when he attacks a critic for dismissing creole as difficult; the
effort required of those who know no creole is rewarding, but it
does require an effort, and this makes the reception of *Slave Song*
self-limiting amongst a diversified poetry readership. The address

of *Coolie Odyssey* is, however, available to the heterogeneous poetry-reading communities of the Caribbean, the metropolitan centres and the Anglophone postcolonial world. It is on these combined sources that the poetry depends for its reinscriptions in critical discussion. In a changing situation where critics are increasingly aware of the need for attention to the structural and historical difference of nations and communities, Dabydeen's iconoclastic poems, which foreground their revision of traditional and modernist forms, can now be received on their own terms – as poetry that estranges customary English usage, returning the language to readers as the bearer of alternative meanings. Because the poetry redraws the map of territory charted by an European cartography, it has the capacity to change the consciousness of its audience.

Notes

1   Colin MacCabe, 'Broken English', *Critical Quarterly*, Vol. 28, No's 1 and 2, p.12.

2   *Decolonising the Mind: The Politics of Language in African Literature*, (London: James Currey, 1986) p.15.

3   'What is a Minor Literature?', in *Kafka: Toward a Minor Literature*, (Minneapolis: University of Minnesota Press, 1986. Published in French, 1975). The argument has been explored and expanded in issues of *Cultural Critique*.

4   Homi Bhabha, 'Representation and the Colonial Text: A Critical Exploration of Some Forms of Mimeticism, in *The Theory of Reading*, (Sussex: Harvester Press, 1984) p.98.

5   Frederic Jameson, 'Third World Literature in the Era of Multi-national Capitalism', *Social Text*, 15 Fall 1986, p.65. For a discussion on the theoretical framework for a 'Third World Literature', see George M Gugelberger, 'Decolonising the Mind: Towards a Theory of Third World Literature'; to be published; and Abdul R. Mohamed, *Manichean Aesthetics: The Politics of Literature in Colonial Africa*, (Amherst: University of Massachusetts Press, 1983).

6   See *The Black Presence in English Literature*, ed. David Dabydeen, (Manchester, Manchester University Press), 1985; *Hogarth's Blacks. Images of Blacks in Eighteenth Century English Art*, (Denmark and

U.K.: Dangaroo Press and Manchester University Press, 1986); *Hogarth, Walpole and Commercial Britain*, (London: Hansib, 1987).

7   In *The State of the Language*, ed. Christopher Ricks, (Berkeley: University of California Press, 1989).

8   Henry Louis Gates, ed *Black Literature and Literary Theory*, (New York and London: Methuen, 1984) p.4.

9   *Black Skin, White Masks* (London: Pluto Press, 1986), with a Foreword by Homi Bhabha; published in French 1952, first English edition, 1967.

10 See Notes to 'The Canecutter's Song' where Dabydeen writes: "She wants to be degraded secretly (the long lace frock is temptingly rich, and it hangs loose, suggestively; also the chaos of her hair), to be possessed and mutilated in the mud. The tragedy is as much hers for her desires too are prevented by social barriers." p.53.

11 *Colonial Encounter: Europe and the Native Caribbean* 1492-1797, (London and New York: Methuen, 1986) p.3.

CHAPTER IV

RESISTANCE AND COMPLICITY IN
DAVID DABYDEEN'S *THE INTENDED*

MARGERY FEE

On his last day in his grandparents' village in Guyana, the narrator of David Dabydeen's *The Intended* is given money and a fare-
well kiss by Auntie Clarice, who calls out 'a final riddle: "you is
we, remember, you is we"'(p.40). This is the riddle the novel sets
out to solve; it is concerned both with the act of memory itself and
with how the highly educated narrator of such a novel can remember properly someone like Auntie Clarice, who is "as old as the
village and . . . as black as the trench water in which every day of
her life she dipped her bucket and took to the house to wash pans,
scrub floors, bathe children" (p.39). Dabydeen sets the problem
out from the perspective of a fiction writer living in Britain:

> The pressure now is also towards mimicry. Either you drop
> the epithet "black" and think of yourself as a "writer" (a few
> of us foolishly embrace this position, desirous of the status
> of "writing" and knowing that "black" is blighted) – that is,
> you cease dwelling on the nigger/tribal/nationalistic theme,
> you cease *folking* up the literature, and you become "univer-
> sal" – or else you perish in the backwater of small presses,
> you don't get published by the "quality" presses, and you
> don't receive the corresponding patronage of media-hype.
> ('On Not Being Milton', p.12-13).

The process of forgetting, in other words, is aided not only by distance, education and time, but also by the way the British literary institution works, by what it publishes, what it valorizes. To remember Auntie Clarice is to risk literary obscurity.

David Dabydeen's family left Guyana in the later 1960s when he was twelve. In England he grew up "in the care of the local authorities, because my parents were divorced"; he remarks of this period in his life that "if you don't have a measure of self-discipline you are finished. It is as bleak as that"[1]. His novel, clearly autobiographical, focuses on a struggling group of young immigrants whose lives were "messy," whose "families [were] scattered across the West", who "lived from hand to mouth, hustling or thieving or working nightshifts and sleeping daytime . . . ashamed of our past, frightened of the present and not daring to think about the future" (p.168). The narrator's father abandons his family in Guyana, but later asks that his son be sent to join him in London; shortly, the father turns his son over to welfare. Desperately, the son studies to succeed, to follow the route traced out for him by Auntie Clarice: "But you must tek education . . . you hear . . . and pass plenty exam and work hard and get good job" (p.38).

The narrator's main aspiration is to write, despite the anxiety of influence he suffers as he studies Milton and Blake for his examinations. His first poem is an epitaph 'published' on the gravestone of his landlord's sister, recently arrived from Pakistan. In the scene where he reads a draft of the epitaph aloud, the narrator knows "it was all wrong" and starts declaiming *Lycidas* to "drown the banality of what I had written" (p.146).

The novel itself is similar, its form analogous to the collage documentary that Joseph, a friend of the narrator's, proposes to make on the condition of England with his stolen video camera. The novel is both 'messy' and under the erasure of the vast weight and privilege of the canon as well as the narrator's tendency to lose faith in books and in words that provide "only the illusion of

truth" (p.197). Nonetheless, its form is not easily labelled
postmodern.[2] For one thing, the surface of the novel is quite realist and it can be read without necessarily grappling with the narrative structure, held together as it is by fairly traditionally
developed character, theme, image, and *Bildungsroman* plot. Further, its structural peculiarities derive not from an international
style or theory, but from a profound although tortured identification with blackness and from the tense/aspect system of the creole
'Nation language' of Guyana. This structure ultimately helps to
ground not only the novel's considerable narrative irony, but also
the constantly uncertain and shifting loyalties of the young narrator in a way that reveals the implied author's allegiance to a
Guyanese and West Indian black identity. The explicit focus of
the novel is on the young narrator's desire to assimilate, to succeed in British terms by going to Oxford, becoming a famous
writer, and marrying an upper-class white woman. This theme is
undercut mainly by irony and structural disjunctions in a way that
problematizes this desire by revealing it as the construct of racist
discourse and racist institutions that permit only a token few
members of racial minorities to succeed. The boy's struggle to jet-
tison his shameful past is retroactively reconstructed by his older
self in a way that re-visions his past, both in Guyana and in the
slums of Balham, as valuable, as worth memorializing. The novel
situates itself as postcolonial text rather than as aspirant to the
British canon by "folking" up the novel form. Its narrative gradually turns the reader's attention away from the hero's struggle to
become white to his subsequent struggle to become black, a move
that transforms the novel into an allegory of the postcolonial immigrant's rejection of imperial norms, a rejection informed by
education, in this case at Oxford, one of the empire's central institutions. As Stephen Slemon puts it in his 'Post-Colonial Allegory and the Transformation of History,' by "foregrounding the
fact that history is not a set of immovable past achievements but a
discourse, open, as are all discursive practices, to reinterpreta-

tion, postcolonial allegorical narratives show that allegorical transformation can also be an effective means of subverting imperial myths".[3] Thus what can be read as a self-punishing recollection of cultural betrayal should also be read as a liberatory account of resistance in desperate circumstances.

Like many other such portraits of the artist as a young man, *The Intended* is marked by the irony of the speaker who has spent years of "solitary hours in Oxford university library" (p.195), a narrator who is no longer a "complete virgin" admiring his friend's "erudition" (p.3) about sex. This ironic doubling implicit in an older narrator's account of a younger self is commonplace in first-person fictionalized autobiography. But in postcolonial novels doubling is more widespread than this. Frequently, such texts "write back" to the imperial canon, revising, resisting, recoding. Dabydeen puts it like this: "You had to take what was defined as English high culture and try to find yourself in there . . . to insert your blackness there".[4] Further, texts written by postcolonial writers who are immigrants to the centre and yet, as the result of racial difference, are doomed to what Arnold Itwaru calls "multiple" and "permanent outsider-ships" also frequently "write back" home, to the former colony.[5] Thus the desire to disappear into an international (that is, imperial) style is complicated by the narrator's inability to forget Auntie Clarice in Guyana, or his East Indian schoolmates like Patel, who speaks for the Balham Asian community: "It's us lot who have given you everything, and don't you forget that" (p.231). Not only must the exiled postcolonial writer produce strong rewritings of (or strong resistance to) the British canonical greats, but he must also produce work that might be read by Patel's children or Auntie Clarice's grandchildren, and that might do justice to the Caribbean theoretical and literary tradition of George Lamming and Wilson Harris as well.

The difficulty of writing to Auntie Clarice is complicated further: Auntie Clarice is descended from African slaves while the narrator is descended from Indian indentured labourers; the two groups have traditionally been opposed in Guyana, with the Indo-Guyanese, although slightly more than half the population, the disadvantaged group. The narrator's mother is negative about the Afro-Caribbeans: "Coolie people had no future in Guyana, she was convinced . . . the black people were so tribal . . . Slavery dirty up their mind" (p.238). When he asks his grandmother, "Ma, is true all black people ignorant?" (p.127), however, she scolds him and makes him wash his mouth out. His rural grandmother lives with her black neighbours in harmony; his mother feels more threatened, living as she does in a town during the troubles between the two groups in the 1960s. Leonard B Glick outlines the complexity of Indo-Guyanese and Afro-Guyanese relations and comments that the choice for the former to identify as black is "essentially a political statement". He continues:

> Many progressive Blacks in Trinidad and Guyana especially would undoubtedly welcome East Indians who ... opted ... for Black identity as affirmation of a political stance. But, for reasons that I have outlined here, that does not seem to be in the offing for the majority of East Indians ... For despite all attempts to integrate East Indians into the story of Caribbean colonialism, the fact remains that they were late comers to the scene, possessed of a distinctive culture of their own, and that they were oppressed and despised by both Whites and Blacks.[6]

Dervla Murphy notes that in Britain "if you are 'politically aware' . . . everyone who is not White is Black," regardless of cultural background or skin colour. She feels that this terminology can obscure important differences, and notes that "most Asians" in Britain "resent being described as 'Blacks'".[7] She has to admit, however, that the identification "Asian" also obscures important differences, particularly for Indo-West Indians. In both situations, Guyanese and British, for someone of Indian ancestry to identify as Black is not only a political decision, but also a decision fraught with tension, since it may not be welcomed by Blacks and may be seen by Asians as a betrayal.

Patel's situation in *The Intended* is at least as complicated as the narrator's; although the narrator has serious disagreements with him, Patel claims the narrator as part of the Balham Asian community, just as Auntie Clarice claims him for Albion village. Patel's family was forced out of Uganda by General Amin in the early 1970s. The Indians in Uganda were brought in by the British before Independence to provide a 'buffer zone' between Whites and Blacks. Not surprisingly, they were likely to share the anti-Black sentiment of the colonialists which secured their monopoly as small shopkeepers, traders, and businessmen against Black competition. After Independence the widespread control of small business by Indians aroused a nationalist resentment fuelled by racism. Patel, however bigoted against Whites he may be, is far less likely to ally himself with Blacks than is the narrator, an "Indian West-Indian Guyanese" (p.5). Deployed as cogs in the machine of imperial trade and commerce, the peoples represented by the narrator's various friends come to Britain bearing the internal scars of their forced moves. They are certainly marked, as are their white oppressors, by a pervasive discourse of racism, although their resistance to it in the case of their own communities has the potential to cause them to realize its wider oppressive function.

The narrator has been shifted through so many different cross-racial situations and discourses that he is, paradoxically, at an advantage in seeing race as a discursive construct. He has himself moved from being a potential victim of Black violence in urban Guyana, through close community connections with Auntie Clarice and other Blacks in rural Guyana, to a Britain where Asians, however marginalized, are higher on the British-constructed racial hierarchy than Blacks. His Asian friends all see

British society through the lens of the discourses of race that
marked their different pasts, discourses that sometimes accord
with, and at other times conflict with, those the narrator brings
with him from the West Indies or learns at school. At the intersec-
tions of these discourses, the narrator is caught in what Wilson
Harris calls the "fabric of the imagination" where one has access
to "revisionary potential within texts of reality" and where one
can situate resistance to the "concepts of invariant identity [that]
function in the modern world as a block imperative at the heart of
cultural politics".[8]

The novel certainly problematizes racial and cultural identification. The narrator's schoolfriends, Nasim, Shaz, and Patel are
described as "the regrouping of the Asian diaspora in a South
London schoolyard" (p.5). Somewhat like a school essay answer-
ing a request for a discussion of similarities and difference, the
novel, having briefly brought these fragments of the diaspora together, proceeds to demonstrate how different they all are. Nasim
is Muslim and speaks Urdu; Shaz speaks only English and although of Muslim background "had never seen the interior of a
mosque" (p.5); Patel speaks Gujarati and is of Hindu background. The narrator's great-great-grandfather "converted to Pres-
byterianism" and "each Friday, to the disgust of Hindu and
Muslim alike, he slaughtered a cow and a pig" (p.69), defying
equally the two major religious traditions of his ancestral homeland. The narrator speaks standard English and an almost-forgot-
ten Creole, and feels guilty about not attending church. The story
of each boy's background, appearance, habits, skills, failures, and
fate makes it clear how limited any view of racial/cultural groups
as uniform must finally be. It is hardly surprising that the narrator
almost despairs of making sense of his life:

> I never really knew any of them anyway, time moved so
> quickly and I was never in one secure place long enough to
> form perfect conclusions . . . All I want is to escape from

this dirt and shame called Balham, this coon condition, this
ignorance that prevents me from knowing anything, not even
who we are, who they are. (p.230)

What he certainly has learned by this point is that whatever the
historical complexities of his own cultural situation, to the majority of British people he is simply Other, part of a mass of inferior
and exploitable flesh.

Although the young narrator often ignores or misinterprets the
significance of what is happening around him to save himself from
despair, the older narrator reveals the pernicious effects of racial
hierarchy in both Guyana and England. The young boy swings
from internal emotional alliances with Indianness and against it;
both moves reveal how he has internalized the discourse of British
racism. Faced with Nasim who has been hospitalized after a beating by Whites and who is surrounded by his weeping and horrified family, he can only identify with the Whites in the ward,
echoing even their slang ("right sight"): "No doubt [Nasim's fam-
ily] presented a right sight to the white patients and guests who
kept eyeing them" (p.15). He continues:

> I knew then that I was not an Asian but that these people
> were yet my kin and my embarrassment. I wished that I were
> invisible. It was the same feeling of shame that all of us,
> whether Indo-West Indians or real Indians, felt at the sight
> of our own people. (p.15)

Later, however, on a bus filled with young Blacks coming from
discos and parties, he allies himself with his Indian heritage:

> No wonder they're treated like animals, I heard myself
> thinking, distancing myself from all this noisy West-Indian-
> ness, and feeling sympathy for the outnumbered whites.
> They should send them back home. All they do is dance and
> breed. Not one 'O' level between a bus-load of them and yet

they complain they've got no jobs, no proper housing, no future. If they stayed home and studied, they'd get somewhere. (p.177)

Again he uses phrases typical of the white discourse of racism against those with which he might be identified. He continues: "I hope the whites can . . . separate me from that lot. I'm an Indian really, deep down I'm decent and quietly spoken and hard-working and I respect good manners, books, art, philosophy. I'm like the whites, we both have civilization" (p.178). When one of the black West Indian boys on the bus offers him a cigarette, however, he feels "deeply ashamed of himself": "everything was so complicated, all this sudden hate and sudden companionship" (p.179). When he feels his Indian heritage held in contempt, he wants to be invisible; when he feels his West Indian heritage, a predominantly Black cultural tradition, under similar pressure, he wants to be Asian. Black is at the bottom of the social hierarchy and he cannot see any way of identifying with it that does not threaten his fragile enterprise of self-construction.

Despite their differences, however, Shaz, Patel, Joseph, and the narrator are all types of Caliban, aiming to steal Prospero's books to get his power. Shaz chooses porn magazines as his books, pimps for Monica, a white girl, and concludes: "Everything in this country is about money ... You don't want to be a Paki all your life" (p.179). Shaz's "new fluency" in sexual explicitness and metaphor is "a complete transformation from his previous stumbling over the English language as represented in our Chaucer and Conrad examination texts" (p.172). He and Patel both choose to challenge the system through crime, exploiting the weakness of whites for sex, pornography, and drugs. Patel says: "All they have over us is money ... Soon we'll have more than them, and England will be one tribe of Patels" (pp.245-46). He has the relation between power, money, and eventual respectability clear: "English people will have names like Lucinda Patel and Egbert Smyth-

Patel" (p.236). After all, nineteenth-century British aristocrats happily married off their impoverished sons to the American daughters of early capitalist robber barons. Patel speculates that money, as much as education, will admit hitherto despised immigrants into the circles of aristocratic privilege, represented by names like "Lucinda," "Egbert," and "Smythe." Thus he has chosen a particular kind of book to steal, "the real kind of book, nowadays".

> His business plan banished all wildness, removed the animal claw and fang, replaced them with colourless, neutral integers, yet I knew instinctively that the latter were more dangerous, that the sums and figures were more threatening, that they could lock you away in prison for the rest of your life, or give you the power to crush heads, obtain whatever or whoever you wanted or willed, the most beautiful and inaccessible of women falling greedily upon your lap, the gold in their teeth flashing as they opened their mouths. (p.201)

Both Shaz and Patel, refused entry into mainstream commerce, take the approach of fighting back, of turning the materialist drive of the culture that refuses them status against that culture.

The narrator and Joseph are idealistic. Joseph "had become Rastafari and all he wanted to do was to learn black history and spread love and feelings to everybody," even though he knows this will not save him from arrest: "If you talk peace, they think you only smoking weed" (p.87). The narrator has already been infected with a belief in the power of literacy and education in Guyana. He must become an educated professional to succeed in the eyes of his family and his Guyanese community. Money alone is not enough.

Although Joseph and the narrator prefer a less materialistic approach than Shaz or Patel, they aim at getting what Pierre Bourdieu calls "symbolic power" in the form of intellectual or artistic skills. Both want to change the white world by their art and get recognition for it; to do so they must enter the white cultural marketplace. The narrator and Joseph are alike in their desires; they both want to "be somebody" (p.113). Both easily slump into self-hatred, into seeing themselves as "useless," as "nothing," because it is clear that no one, even those paid to protect and educate them, will actually recognize their potential or help them succeed. Joseph says, "all the time they seeing you as animal, riot, nigger, but you know you is nothing, atoms, only image and legend in their minds" (p.101). Joseph steals the video camera because, as he says, "I can't read nor write but I can see" (p.107): for him the camera is "a different kind of book" (p.105). The young narrator feels less optimistic: "[Joseph] was, after all, genuinely incompetent ... full of unrealistic half-formed ideas which he didn't have the resources to develop. Everything was contained in books and he was handicapped by illiteracy" (p.107).[9] After Joseph commits suicide the narrator can see him only as a negative example, since he clearly fears that he too will fail in his attempt at gaining recognition as an individual, rather than as a stereotype. He chooses another White book to steal, the British literary canon, even though he fears that "all this reading of books and effort at learning will lead nowhere" (p.179).

Two emotional relationships central to the narrator's struggle to construct an identity for himself are those he forges with the white, upper-class Janet and with Joseph. In a sense they map out the bleak opposition that the dominant stereotypes force on those categorized as Other: assimilate (and, implicitly, vanish into the majority) or just vanish into the shadows of the margin. As Dabydeen put it in a comment about his generation in England: as the result of the public hostility to immigrants there was "a very great pressure among us to become invisible".[10] At Oxford, then, the narrator believes he will be transformed into someone worthy of Janet: "I will have become somebody definite, my education compensating for my colour in the eyes of her parents" (p.245). He worries about his motives: "Patel's taunt that I want to become a white man is ridiculous" (p.230), but he is so powerless that he has few choices. Joseph becomes an image of Blackness against which the narrator feels compelled to define himself, even though he feels pressures to assert their common 'West Indianness.' Nonetheless, he concludes, "the most important thing is to save myself from the misery of his kind of being" (p.231).

It is in the crossing of the dangerous frontiers of gender, race, and class necessary for the narrator to construct relationships with these two where the dangers of complicity with the dominant discourse are the greatest. And yet, as Kenneth Ramchand makes clear, it is across just such frontiers that West Indian writers must move to achieve any form of true community. Speaking of (and quoting from) Wilson Harris, he writes:

> Instead of creating characters whose positioning on one side or other of the region's historical conflicts consolidates those conflicts and does violence to the make-up of the person, the West Indian novelist should set out to 'visualize a fulfilment,' a reconciliation in the person and throughout society, of the parts of a heritage of broken cultures.[11]

Dabydeen certainly does not see reconciliation as an easy achievement: all the non-White characters in the novel are, in a sense, deformed by the pressures of racism (as are Monica and Janet to differing degrees, by the pressures of sexism) and their chances of reconciliation with others is strongly dependent on their background and personal history.

The young narrator clearly cannot detach Janet from his fantasy of her stable privileged family life or Joseph from fears of failing, of falling even further down the social hierarchy; the older narrator is able to allow them their own original and compelling voices. But in their relations to the novel's thematic structure, they nonetheless remain counters in a working out of binary oppositions. The White woman and the Black man become poles between which the narrator seeks to find himself, their abstract quality made clear by Joseph's death and Janet's departure for Australia. One of Dabydeen's own poems, 'Caliban' outlines the dilemma from the perspective of the coolie Caliban, loved by a White woman:

> The first night
> I endured your creation
>
> . . .
>
> You were always bountiful with fantasy,
> Fashioning me your Image or casting me Native
> (*Coolie Odyssey*), p.34.

It is difficult, maybe impossible, not to use those defined as Other in ways that suit one's own needs for a public identity.

In contrast, the narrator's relations with his South Asian friends are less schematic and less fraught with anxiety. Shaz helps him achieve what he regards as sexual maturity and Patel helps him financially. Nasim's mother worries over him. He is grateful for these evidences of concern, but accepts them as one would similar favours from a family member. Nasim's sister, unlike Janet or Monica, is classified as family; to sleep with her "would have been like sleeping with a sister" (p.212). The narrator's disagreements with these friends are just that, rather than symbolic of larger social conflicts. These relationships do not pose the threat of those that must bridge discursive dichotomies or defy the dominant discourse.

Janet, for example, is using her relationship with the narrator to distinguish herself from her family, and certainly as an exercise of power, since he, unlike someone like Shaz, is prepared to let her take the lead sexually. Because of their differences of race and class, their relationship is charged with the potential for disaster for both of them. He consents to her desire to keep their relationship secret from her parents until he graduates: "I will be her dark secret, her illicit pregnancy, her undeveloped child" (p.245). Thus in his view she becomes dominant like his mother or his grandmother. Just before he leaves for Oxford and she for Australia, Janet fits him out in a white shirt which he is to wear when they meet again; it has unfortunate connotations for the narrator, whose father wore a similar shirt, beating his wife when she could not get the ink stains off the pocket. (This is an allusion to the "starched collars and got-up shirt fronts" of the Company's chief accountant in Conrad's *Heart of Darkness*, which may well have depended on a similar oppression of the native woman who "had a distaste for the work" of doing laundry). As Janet pulls at the sleeves to check the fit, the narrator says, "I felt like one of Shaz's whores, or a slave on an auction block" (p.243). With her, he is feminized, objectified, infantilized and sexually ashamed. This is the effect of the white culture she symbolizes on the black Other.

Janet also becomes symbolic both of the alma mater and its gatekeepers; when the narrator attempts to penetrate her, he finds the entrance "unmanageably small" (p.203). He does not attempt to rape this Miranda, nor can he even make love to her. He is symbolically represented as not yet her equal. The text awaits his transformation by Oxford just as he does. After this failure, he feels "uselessness" (p.204). Janet seems unruffled, however, and asks him when his interview is at Oxford and what he will talk about: "Pretend I'm the board of scholars and you are sitting before me"(p.205). She has quickly transformed herself from passive virgin to dominant mistress, taking on the role of the gatekeeper of white culture. Indeed, her class background and her colour, if not her gender, entitle her to this culture almost by right. Asked to define poetry, the narrator says: "It's like a seed, according to Shelley, containing the past and future plant" (p.205). Given his recent failure, the connections are obvious, and Janet replies:

> Well, I suppose it depends on what kind of plant – either a
> sissy daffodil or a Venus fly-trap. I bet Shelley was thinking
> of daffodils. Men always go for vulnerable images, things
> they can control and dominate. Me, I think poetry is a meat-
> eating, cunning flower that traps your tongue and won't let
> go. (p.205)

Suddenly evoking images of the *vagina dentata*, she turns the
muse into "la belle sans merci" relentlessly trapping and dis-
carding men. As she leaves, she smilingly and ironically says,
"Well, do your best in Oxford and make sure you get in this time"
(p.205). Here, although she has been given her own voice, one
that reveals her originality, wit and power, she is clearly also being 'used' for artistic reasons in the narrative. Just as she might
prove a dangerous muse for the narrator, so might Oxford leave
him 'death pale,' assimilated, unable to write. As the novel draws
to an end, the narrator begins to see his relationship with Janet in
less idealistic terms. When he blurts out his desire – "but you
are fragrant, you are everything I intended," – he realizes how his
feelings for her have not, in fact, been intended, but have been
forced by his "plain needs" and "weakness" (p.243). Patel puts it
more crudely: "Just because you ain't got a mother don't mean
that England will mother you, you stupid mother-fucker... Why
don't you grow up and be yourself instead of mourning for white
pussy?" (p.246). In his relationship with Janet, issues of race and
class will always disrupt any attempt to construct their relationship in terms of intracultural norms of friendship or sexual part-
nership. She stands for England, for Oxford, for white privilege
just as Joseph stands for the West Indies, for Borstal, for black
oppression.

It is the memory of Joseph that has the potential, at least, to
break down the young narrator's idealization of British culture.
Joseph kills himself because the only work he can find using his
camera is filming pornography for Patel and he cannot bear it: he

is "fed up with filth" (p.234). The narrator tries to convince him
that "it's not the subject, it's the technique that matters, perfect-
ing your knowledge of how the camera works, and how you can
make it work for you" (p.234), but Joseph' reaction makes it clear
that this approach is wrong. To abstract subject from technique is
to transform art into exploitation. The young narrator tries to convince Patel to continue to help Joseph, even after Joseph has deliberately ruined a film, and rebukes Patel for his racism in
Auntie Clarice's words: "there's no need to call him a nigger.
He's one of us and we're one of him" (p.240). Nonetheless, he
himself still sees Joseph as inferior: "perhaps he wanted to burn
like a Hindu corpse to show us Asians that he was no different
from us, that he was not an inferior being, that 'you is we,' as
Auntie Clarice had said" (p.197). Even after the narrator is at
Oxford, "the memory of Joseph, an inveterate criminal, keeps
breaking in to the most burglar-proof of institutions, reminding
me of my dark shadow, drawing me back to my dark self"
(pp.195-96). But the narrator's reaction is still revulsion: "I begin to despise Joseph, his babbling, his half-formed being, his
lack of privilege, his stupid way of living and dying" (p.198). He
sees Joseph as the antithesis of everything he has been trained to
value by white education. He "long[s] to be white, to be calm, to
write with grace and clarity, to make words which have status"
(p.197) and is convinced that Oxford will transform him into
someone who can do this. Here the danger of forgetting one's people, of forgetting one's own history, of thinking it belongs, like
other remnants of Balham, in the "bins" (p.210) is made clear.

In fact, the text plays with the possibility that the narrator
might indeed have forgotten Joseph in the section of the novel
that goes farthest into the future of any other section (although,
typically, it is found in the first third of the book). The narrator
recollects having his car repaired in a garage which resembles
Joseph's description of his father's but when he begins to ask
whether the man had a son called Joseph, he forgets Joseph's

family name, which is, significantly, "Countryman." As Marlow's fascination with Kurtz focuses *Heart of Darkness,* so the narrator's fascination with Joseph becomes a moral test. The narrator's forgetting is like Marlow's lie to Kurtz's intended, a revelation of the difficulty of facing the horror of what the social hierarchy can do to the weak. Marlow's gradual realization that Kurtz is, in fact, far from a model, works for the narrator in reverse. Joseph, whom the young narrator often sees as unhinged, impractical and incoherent, is shown by the older narrator to have much better developed political, poetic, and critical insights than the young narrator had himself. Like the narrator's first poem, this novel also becomes an elegy for a dead person of colour, although its elegiac qualities only become clear retrospectively.[12] The narrator does save himself from vanishing like Joseph and his novel saves Joseph from dying unmemorialized. Further, Joseph's memory saves the narrator from going white, from vanishing into the heart of whiteness, from rebirth out of the womb of Oxford as Janet's "medieval knight" (p.244), completely assimilated into white bourgeois gentility.

Benita Parry has expressed concern that Dabydeen's poems in *Slave Song* may be implicated in a "discourse shared by the master's culture and beyond," in this case a sexist discourse "that represents rape as what woman wants," because the "pain, frustration and anger is spoken by the native positioned as the very figure of phobic white fears and desires".[13] The greater flexibility of characters who speak out of multiple and conflicting discourses lessens this danger in *The Intended,* although ultimately, since there is no "outside" to discourse, it is impossible to avoid complicity at some level with some dominant and oppressive discourse. Dabydeen shows characters, including the youthful subject of the narrative, overwhelmed by racist discourse, either turning their resulting anger outward at both whites and blacks, or inward on themselves in the form of self-doubts, even suicidal self-loathing. For the narrator, the solution ("tek education")comes both with the risk of assimilation and complicity, and the potential to use that education to produce resistance, ("remember"). Thus he takes both of Auntie Clarice's pieces of advice to heart. The final text is an example of how an assimilative education can be turned against assimilation, can be used to provide the confidence and power to look again at the past, to describe the process of oppression, to scrutinize past cultural betrayals in painful detail. And the novel's crucial remembering of the West Indian culture symbolized by both Joseph and Auntie Clarice takes place not only in the novel's content, but also in the ways its form can be linked to Creole.

Guyanese Creole has been seen by writers such as Wordsworth McAndrew and Herbert Devonish as a means to provide Afro-and Indo-Guyanese with a unified national identity that would promote political equality in two groups deliberately kept at odds by the colonial master: "each group was encouraged to share the planters' disparaging stereotypes of the other".[14] Thus its use in *The Intended* is as much a gesture towards Guyanese cross-racial solidarity as it is in Dabydeen's paired poetry collections, *Slave Song* (1984) and *Coolie Odyssey* (1988). In fact, its use is a gesture towards West Indian unity, since related creoles are spoken throughout the Caribbean. In *The Intended,* it can be argued that the use of Creole, not only in dialogue but also in the narrative structure, serves to valorize those of Joseph's views that annoyed and appalled the young narrator, obsessed with his drive for completion, perfection, and clarity.

The young narrator, waiting to leave for Oxford, remembers a "haphazard" letter from his mother, written "in a struggling English, the verb-tenses mixed up so that I couldn't figure past from present from future" (p.213), and a little later wonders: "Perhaps I am not English enough: a piece of pidgin, not knowing where the past ended, where the present began, not knowing how the future was to be made" (pp.216-17). In Guyanese Creole, as in many other such languages, "tense marking is optional".[15] What is marked grammatically is aspect, that is, broadly, whether an action is complete at the time of speaking or whether the action is continuing. In much the same way as Creole, the novel generally ignores tense, instead promoting the imperfective over the perfective aspect.

A careful look at the time sequence of the novel reveals that the narrative slides between Guyanese past, Balham present and, although rarely, Oxford future, even in the short sections within chapters that are simply marked off by white spaces. The same is true of the book's four long chapters, which are marked off with Roman numerals. The first chapter begins in Balham, and gives an account of the first day at school in England, but is devoted mainly to an account of the narrator's last day with his grandparents before he leaves Guyana. Both of these accounts move around in time, however, with interpolated stories, memories, and digressions. In each subsequent chapter, the narrator has aged and his relationships with his friends have changed, but no section lacks a passage set in the Guyanese past. In other words, its influence is continuing, despite the narrator's feeling that he is forgetting his past. One particularly significant story recurs, that of Shaz and the narrator taking food to Joseph in a condemned and abandoned house, first after he has escaped from jail where he has been taken for stealing the video camera, and later after he has fled from his job filming porn for Patel. Versions of this encounter recur (pp. 88, 164, 166, 170, 193, 234) and in each instance Joseph's dejection, depression, and filthiness and the narrator's feelings of helplessness increase. This compulsive repetition indicates both the narrator's guilt about Joseph's death and that this event is incomplete – Joseph will continue to haunt the text and the narrator. In grammatical terms, Joseph's aspect is marked as continuative. The narrator, sitting in the library at Oxford, remembers a scene where Joseph had been trying to learn to write "cocoon" on the muddy floor of his hideout:

I see Joseph's stick gouging letters in the mud, the sense of which now comes to me fitfully. He was telling me that he was half-formed, like the jelly in a cocoon, like the C trying to round itself to an O, getting there with great effort, but breaking up because of the police, the Boy's Home, the absent father, the dead mother, the lack of education, the poverty, the condition of blackness. Even the quest for completion was absurd, for O signified nothing, the word ended with N for nothing. (p.196)

The narrator's response at this point is to yearn for completion: "I will grow strong in this library, this cocoon, I will absorb its nutrients of quiet scholarship, I will emerge from it and be somebody, some recognizable shape, not a lump of aborted anonymous flesh" (p.198). That he does not forget Joseph, that he is not reborn a white "somebody," however, is finally made clear in the structure of the text, which mimics not the rational order enforced by Standard English and "essayist literacy,"[16] but the apparently haphazard one of Creole. Joseph "had a way of rambling, never getting to the point" (p.88), and the novel finally commemorates and celebrates this refusal.[17] Joseph, after all, expresses throughout the book his poetic and visionary interpretations of life, language, literature, and the condition of England, interpretations that reveal the sterility of the "theme and image" approach favoured by the narrator, not to mention that of his uncritical attempts to become white. Joseph sees what the young narrator cannot, but the older narrator dares to:

Poetry is like bird ... and it gliding or lifting and plunging ... What you doing with your pentating and strokee and all dem rules is putting iron-bar one by one in a spacious room so the bird flying round and round and breaking beak and wing against the wall trying to reach the sunlight. You turning all the room in the universe and in the human mind into bird cage. (p.95)

The text itself, in its form, its deliberate messiness, counters the iron cage of racial absolutism and hierarchy, the dominance of Standard English, and the ideal of clarity, order, and homogeneous identity, moving the reader back to Wilson Harris's "revisionary potential": "an active and infinite ingredient within imageries and texts of reality – to which one responds intuitively at many levels, ... [a response that implies] the ecstasy of complex counterpoint within a living medium, a changing language: complex counterpoint between partial origins, between partial imprints of unfinished genesis, partial absolutes".[18] At the end of the novel, the young narrator departs for Oxford, hoping to learn there how to form "perfect conclusions." By this point, the reader has already learned that the belief in perfect conclusions is fostered by oppressive ideologies that turn the wide world into an iron cage.

Notes

1   Interview with Wolfgang Binder. *Journal of West Indian Literature 3.2* (1989), 67-80.

2   The novel itself is a complex intertext, something I have only been able to gesture at here. If it is to be considered postmodern as a result, its explicit focus on texts that obsess postcolonial writers in their political project, such as Shakespeare's *The Tempest* and Conrad's *Heart of Darkness*, as well as on postcolonial works such as Wilson Harris's *Palace of the Peacock*, certainly distinguishes it from the postmodern writing of American, British, and European writers.

3   Stephen Slemon. 'Post-Colonial Allegory and the Transformation of History', *Journal of Commonwealth Literatures* 23.1 (1988): 157-67.

4   Interview with Binder, *op.cit.*, p.72.

5   Arnold Itwaru, 'Exile and Commemoration', *Indenture and Exile: The Indo-Caribbean Experience.* Ed. Frank Birbalsingh. (Toronto: TSAR, 1989), pp. 202-6.

6   Leonard B Glick, 'Epilogue: The Meanings of Ethnicity in the Caribbean', in *Ethnicity Revisited.* A Special Issue of *Ethnic Groups: International Periodical of Ethnic Studies.* Ed. Stephen Glazier (New York: Gordon and Breach, 1985), 149-64.

7   Dervla Murphy, *Tales from Two Cities: Travels of Another Sort,* (London: Penguin, 1987), p.13.

8   Wilson Harris, "The Fabric of the Imagination." *From Commonwealth to Post-Colonial,* Ed. Anna Rutherford, (Sydney: Dangaroo, 1992) p. 16.

9   Harvey Graff's work makes it clear that literacy does not necessarily promote social improvement for those at the bottom of the social hierarchy, although illiteracy is frequently blamed for their position there. (*The Literacy Myth,* New Brunswick: Transaction, 1991).

10   Interview with Binder, *op. cit.,* p.70.

11   Kenneth Ramchand, Preface to 1968 ed. of *Palace of the Peacock,* by Wilson Harris (London: Faber, 1960), p.iii.

12   The novel is clearly a version of what Bruffee identifies as the "elegiac romance," a genre developed by Conrad. A similar point is made by the fact that only the incomplete draft versions of the narrator's epitaph for Mr Ali's sister are found in the text, not the final version that is, presumably, carved on her gravestone. See Kenneth Brufee's *Elegiac Romance, Cultural Change and the loss of The Hero in Modern Fiction,* (Ithaca: Cornell UP, 1983).

13   Benita Parry, 'Between Creole and Cambridge English: The Poetry of David Dabydeen.' In this volume.

14   John R Rickford, *Dimensions of a Creole Continuum: History, Texts, and Linguistic Analyses of Guyanese Creole* (Stanford, CS: Stanford UP, 1987), p.66.

15   See John Roy's essay on creole in Manfred Görlach and John A. Holm, Eds., *Focus on the Caribbean: Varieties of English Around the World,* (Amsterdam: John Benjamins, 1986), p.146.

16   The narrator, schooled in "essayist literacy", cannot appreciate Joseph's orally derived vision of the world. Indeed, their differences are as much differences of consciousness as of race or class.

17   Although the novel celebrates the power of creole, it does not tackle Rasta talk, or "lyric". Joseph does not appear to use it, although he does definitely speak a creole.

18   Wilson Harris, op. cit., p.20.

CHAPTER V

THE INTENDED

BENITA PARRY

Defending the 'Heritage of the Language' is a coded resistance to an English that is being re-invented by its multiple users. It is a sign of the disquiet of a political and intellectual rearguard at the challenge which a polyglot and cosmopolitan migrant population presents to the notion of 'the nation' as an homogenous construct. Hence the quest of David Dabydeen's Guyanese narrator to redefine his identity through producing prose in Standard English can be read as beseeching entry to a community imagined as being culturally and linguistically homogeneous. His is the standard dream of a bygone colonial élite where to write the oppressors' language with proper attention to grammatical and syntactic rules is to be liberated from a colonized condition:

> I suddenly long to be white, to be calm, to write with grace and clarity, to make words which have status, to shape them into the craftsmanship of English china, coaches, period furniture, harpsichords, wigs, English anything, for whatever they put their hands and minds to worked wonderfully. Everything they produced was fine and lasted forever. We are mud, they the chiselled stone of Oxford that has survived centuries and will always be here. (pp.197-8).

To the extent that Dabydeen's *roman a clef* is constrained by the narrator's performance of this aspiration, it resembles the normative apprenticeship novel, the tracing of an irregular route from colonial through immigrant deprivations to a place at Oxford, retaining resonances of already-read scenarios set in different climes and other times. That it turns out to be more than the enactment of his ambition, is due to the narrator inadvertently fracturing the structure which his story seeks to set in place and on which it depends. Thus every prediction written into his chronicle of a journey towards assimilation is interrupted by the very utterances he would denigrate and deny, every move towards the projected goal diverted by voices calling him back from the urge to historical and cultural amnesia.

Many stories are now being told about the postcolonial diaspora in Britain: these are diverse in medium and modes of narration and differentiated by the geographical origins, the cultural, class and occupational positions, the gender and sexual identities of the tellers. Dabydeen's is told by a narrator who is a young heterosexual male, an Indian Guyanese descended from low-caste Hindu indentured labourers, and a parentless schoolboy immigrant in Britain. His is offered as a story of disentitlement, dispossession and lack. About his forebears' homeland he is ignorant: "I had no knowledge whatsoever of India, no inkling of which part my ancestors came from, nor when they left, nor even their names"; of Hindu tradition and ritual he knows little, his great-great-grandfather having converted to Christianity, which itself plays no part in the family's life. His only connection to this discontinuous history and broken past is through his grandmother who wears a thick silver bracelet around her ankle "which had come all the way from India", and who is the bearer of legend and rumour about the family's fortunes and misfortunes in Guyana.

What he does know is that they are Indians, though neither his mother's fears of African-Caribbeans — exacerbated during the race riots on the eve of independence — nor the received wisdom about their propensity to violence and ignorance gets in the way of his learning that the communities are united by a history of enforced migration, share a colonial condition and speak the same language. More than once he returns to his last meeting with Auntie Clarice ("truly she was old, her African face sprouting hairs between the cracks, like a golden apple-seed") who gives him a carefully-saved five-dollar bill and whose parting words, "You is we, remember you is we" later reverberate to arrest his impulse to separation from "noisy West-Indianness".

Deprivation, backwardness, incomprehension, incapacity are recurrent terms in his judgement of urban New Amsterdam and rural Albion Village, and are repeated in his perception of the postcolonial migrants in the rundown suburbs of England. Feeling this way, his desire to make something of himself demands an impossible forgetfulness: "All I want is to escape from this dirt and shame called Balham, this coon condition, this ignorance that prevents me from knowing anything, not even who we are, who they are." Instead his story is an act of remembrance without sentimentality about want, squalid living conditions, and drunkenness in Guyana, but not without reverence for the culture of survival nurtured and sustained by its communities; and even as he withholds value from Creole as the speech of adversity and illiteracy, the vivid and versatile utterances of its speakers are a rebuke to his denials.

His account of black migration in Britain, while not without compassion, anger and wit, is marked by a determined detachment. Where the representation of this diaspora has tended to focus on cultural imbrication – whether effected in a glamorized underworld, amongst sophisticated metropolitans, on the meeting ground of sexual identities and political affiliations, and so on – Dabydeen's social space is situated on the margins. Where other constructions have foregrounded refusal, assertion and affirmation in the redefinition of the migrant experience, Dabydeen's players want invisibility. Of his friend's mother, he observes that only on entering "the protected environment of her house, the doors and curtains closed to alien eyes", its rooms decorated in green,

smelling sweetly of spices, its walls displaying pictures of wor-
shippers in Mecca does "her sari reveal(ed) a grace and dignity."
The status of outsiders which he assigns the community is registered by their insufficiency in English, the shopkeeper's anxiety
about the wording stamped on his passport, "permitted to remain
in the United Kingdom for an indefinite period", a sign of the inability to escape from the immigrant condition: "He would grow
dismal, muttering about how English was so hard, how every word
had a dozen different understandings, how he could barely pro-
nounce the words, never mind glean their multiple meanings".

His is the world of landlords to destitute tenants, open-all-
hours corner grocers, owners of video shops, unskilled labour:

> In the swift journey between Tooting Bec and Balham, we re-
> lived the passage from India to Britain, or India to the
> Caribbean to Britain, the long journeys of a previous century
> across unknown seas towards the shame of plantation
> labour ... families scattered across the west, settling in one
> country or another depending on the availability of visas; we
> lived from hand to mouth, hustling or thieving or working
> nightshifts and sleeping daytime; we were ashamed of our
> past, frightened by the present and not daring to think of the
> future. (pp.17, 168).

If Dabydeen's migrants necessarily inhabit two worlds and are
contributors to the formation of Britain's contemporary protean
cultures, their limited access to English confines them to the
periphery. When their more aggressive children claim citizenship
by becoming amateur pimps, small-time drug-dealers and
inexpert purveyors of pornography, their facility in the foreign
tongue is limited to its most debased forms, whether the inert
jargon of Business Plans or the brutalized vocabulary of sex
magazines, thus again condemning them to the margins.

In the narrator's book then proper English is real power, and he intends to acquire both. The title is borrowed from a canonical work which the underprivileged and ambitious schoolboy is studying for his 'A' Levels; Kurtz's formal designation of his betrothed being used in several of its alternative meanings, as aspiration and as transfiguration. This last is registered in the narrator's recollections of the mosques and temples of Guyana treasured by their users, "their white-washed domes and elegant turrets . . . exhibitions of the beauty and idealism of their barefoot lives." The former is performed by the boy in the care of the Social Services who gets to read English at Oxford. But although it is he who realizes his ambition by formally moving to the official centre – "I am no longer an immigrant here, for I can decipher the texts" – while the illiterate Joseph Countryman destroys himself, it is the visionary Rastafarian who is the novel's figure of a utopian desire. Lacking a command of Standard English but with a capacity to use words appropriate to his exorbitant intentions, Joseph undermines the certainties which the narrator naively avows, his untrained intelligence and untutored imagination a reproach to his friend's eager participation in rites of the educational apparatus. Where the narrator accepts language as a pliant medium to be crafted by skilled users, and elevates writing over all other texts, Joseph knows that "Words are so full of cleverness . . . Every word is cat with nine separate lives", understands that a video camera is "a different kind of book", and obsessed with the word 'cocoon' while in a state of advanced disorientation, struggles to enunciate an inchoate version of how language is a system of meaning constituted by signs that are arbitrary and differential, dependent on conventions and relations:

> They were the very first chaotic attempts he had made in his life to write something, apart from his name . . . 'It's me, all of that is me . . . here is C and this one here is O and another C and two more O's, and then N . . . Look! C is half O .

.. it nearly there, but when it form O it breaking up again,
never completing . . . A is for apple, B for bat, C is for cocoon, which is also coon, N is for nuts, N is for nothing, N is
for nignog. Can't you see, all of it is me. (p.194-95)

While the narrator accedes to the requirements of the English
Literature syllabus, quickly learning to apply the method of
'theme and imagery', 'appearance and reality' to any piece of
writing he studies, Joseph protests at rules putting an iron-bar in
a room where the bird of poetry is trapped, and refuses his
friend's facile explanation that Conrad's blacks dying under the
trees relate to the notion of suffering and redemption at the core
of the novel's concerns:

> No it ain't, is about colours. You been saying is a novel 'bout
> the fall of man, but is really 'bout a dream . . . The white
> light of England and the Thames is the white sun over the
> Congo that can't mix with the green of the bush and black
> skin of the people. All the colours struggling to curve against
> each other like rainbow, but instead the white light wants to
> blot out the black and the green and reduce the world to one
> blinding colour . . . The white man want clear everything
> away, clear away the green bush and the blacks and turn the
> whole place into ivory which you can't plant or smoke or eat.
> Ivory is the heart of the white man. (p.98-9)

In contrast to the narrator's search for recognition by the master culture through assimilation, Joseph withdraws from its gaze,
absenting himself from the identity it would impose on him:

> When I was in borstal I was rumour. They look at me and see
> ape, trouble, fist. And all the time I nothing, I sleep and
> wake and eat like a zombie . . . and no ideas in my mind, no
> ideas about where I come from and where I should be going.
> You can't even see yourself, even if you stand in front of mir-

ror, all you seeing is shape. But all the time they seeing you as animal, riot, nigger, but you know you is nothing, atoms, only image and legend in their minds.

To fashion a self Joseph positions himself as a Rastafarian and looks to Africa, urging the narrator to find a book "which told the whole story" different from the one which said "that we don't have any chemistry and sums . . . That we walk about naked with other people's bones through our noses . . . That we eat each other", and aspiring to register this identity through making a film of *Heart of Darkness* on his stolen video camera.

Thus the identity of Joseph, the graduate of Borstals and Boys' Homes and the speaker of a deviant English, is multilocated, dispersed, creolized, whereas the narrator, who has proved his proficiency as a writer of the stepmother tongue, seeks a refashioning that requires him to deny his native beginnings and migrant experience. At Oxford, long after Joseph's suicide, the narrator is haunted by him "breaking into the most burglar-proof of institutions, reminding me of my dark shadow, drawing me back to my dark self", but determined to remake himself as a figure who can be accommodated in the master narrative – "I will grow strong in this library, this cocoon . . . I will emerge from it and be somebody, some recognisable shape, not a lump of aborted, anonymous flesh."

If the narrator is sometimes earnestly and sometimes acerbically up-front about his susceptibility to the seductions of The English Heritage, and is neither apologetic nor censorious about his shame at being kith and kin to rumbustious West Indians or Asians "wrapped in alien, colourful clothes who whispered to each other in a strange tongue", the incongruity of his intentions are abundantly inscribed. Other ironies emerge contingently, for the paradox of this fiction is that in a text which is preoccupied with language, in which language is cultural artefact and social lever, no shift in linguistic usage is effected.

"Black people have to have their own words." This retort to the
narrator's attempt at a classically-styled epitaph for the obscure
sister of his humble Pakistani landlord, comes from Shaz, inept
student and soon-to-be devourer of pornography, client of prostitutes and pimp, which considerably diminishes its authority. Yet it
is Shaz's observation which haunts the book as reprimand and re-
minder that Europhone colonial and postcolonial writing, in
bringing the experience of colonialism and postcoloniality into
representation, appropriated and overturned tropes and literary
traditions, and invented new hybridized languages as a means of
interrogating and subverting the master culture.

Here, however, a narrator determined to establish his own linguistic competence, consigns Broken English, both the fluent rep-
ertoire of Creole and the eccentric improvisations of recent
migrants, to direct reported speech, while keeping his own
enunciations free of their transgressions. (A very different strategy is deployed by Dabydeen in his poetry). The consequence of
this separation is a fiction which despite its deliberate juxtaposition of temporalities and its crossing of genre boundaries in mix-
ing social and marvellous realism, personal testimony with
detached commentary, does not seek to rupture received fictional
form. Can we attribute this to a complicity between text and narrator? Is this narrator the product or the producer of the text?
That ambiguous area where the critical is embroiled with the con-
fessional is discernible in the representation of sexuality. The
charge of pornography made against the fiction in the *New Statesman and Society* is patently absurd, the stories of adolescent mas-
turbation and failed fumblings so innocent as to be disjunct from
the depiction of erotic behaviour intended to cause sexual excitement. What is, however, disturbing is that the language of a con-
summated encounter is without the affection that is brought to the
remembrance of a childhood in Guyana where the women are not
victims but survivors and actors. Thus although the narrator re-
coils from the clichés of sex magazines and is repelled by Shaz's

disgusted lusting after the female body, he writes of Monica, the apprentice prostitute managed by Shaz, as a commodity that changes hands – "Shaz's parting gift ... She let me take her." Dabydeen has told one of many possible stories about postcolonial migrancy, one in which the narrator, having at the outset made up his mind about his goal, is left on the threshold of adulthood in many minds. Yet I must argue that because the distance between the discourse of text and narrator always shifts and sometimes closes, the critique is enfolded with confession, and confession bears within it the seeds of exculpation. Hence the narrator is not only the object of censure – and a recognizable representative of one route pursued by postcolonial writers whose intentions are interrogated by the fiction – but survives as the voice of an aspiration whose legitimacy has not, in the space of the novel, been displaced.

CHAPTER VI

DISAPPEARANCE

JEAN POPEAU

In David Dabydeen's *Disappearance,* the narrator, a black Guyanese engineer, goes to an English village on the South coast on a project to build a sea-wall as protection for the village. We see the village with its eccentricities and peculiarities through the colonial's eyes. But it is a world which has already constituted him as Other and formulated the terms of his otherness as a black West Indian. The narrator has to negotiate this formulation while engaged in his prospecting of the area, and, something he conceives for himself, a quest for the English, in what might be considered the quintessential English village.

The English village may be said to be the last redoubt and container of the peculiarity which is Englishness. The towns and cities have long become multicultural reflections of various migrations and movements painful to Powellite and Churchillian* psyches. It is the English village which may legitimately claim the rural dreams and aspirations of those Englishmen hankering after a pastoral Eden associated with a certain strain of values encapsulated by 'Englishness'. If the Americans have their wilderness to search for the 'real America', the Englishman seeks for his soul in the village. It is, however, a search which is perhaps rendered ironic by hundreds of years of the reworking of the land, the flattening of contours into similar geometrical areas of farmland (over 95% of England's original woodland has been destroyed) in which the individualities which supposedly characterize 'Englishness' have been progressively buried. The

---

* I am thinking here of Winston Churchill's latest speeches against further immigration.

rural Eden remains a painful area of the psyche made more poignant as the possibilities for its recreation become more remote.

It is one of the many ironies of the novel that it is the colonial Black who is called upon to protect the village and the values it represents, an occupation which allows him the opportunity to seek the essence he unwittingly protects. The colonial who should perhaps be engaged in undermining all such 'essences' as 'Englishness', 'nationhood', 'country' as formulating and imprisoning concepts ranged against his interest, works to protect these values, crystalized in the village, against the ravages of time and nature.

The narrator boards at the home of Mrs Rutherford, a widow who has lived in Africa with Jack, her estranged husband. Her sympathy for Africa and Africans is embodied in a collection of masks she calls her "children". The narrator's comic and enigmatic relations with Mrs Rutherford manifest as challenges to his self-conception as anti-ideological, a 'facts-and-figures man'. Mrs Rutherford constantly returns him to his situation as a colonial with poignant threads connecting him to Africa. The masks manifest ambiguity. Although later he will interpret them differently, early in the narrative they assume a painful burden of historical images:

> They forced me to connect the smudged photograph and Swami's death, and, before that, the rape of Amerindian women, malarial fever, the drowning of my Dutch predecessors and the wastage of slave bodies. These images which I had buried piecemeal in my mind surfaced in a ritual sequence of shame.[1]

The masks form a potent symbol of mystery, piercing, like Mrs Rutherford's eyes, yet harbouring shifting meanings.

The narrator forms a friendship with Christie, one of the work-
men in his project, who partially tells him the story of Curtis, the
eccentric bachelor whom Mrs Rutherford had joined in a cam-
paign to save the village from the sea. Like the narrator, Christie
is an expatriate, an Irishman with a keen sense of his place
amongst the villagers as the clownish outsider. Through him the
narrator can both interpret the otherness of the village and learn
the terms of his own role as preformulated Other. Christie inter-
prets the village's view of him. It is Christie who sheds some
doubt on the narrator's sense of reality with suggestions that Professor Fenwick, his mentor who has recommended him for the job,
might have been implicated, with Rushton, the foreman of the
works, in taking money from the project; that Mrs Rutherford
might have had an affair with the Tory eccentric, Curtis, despite
her left-wing protestations.

Mrs Rutherford's absent husband Jack (after whom her dog is
named) and Curtis are combined together in a mystery which in-
trigues the narrator and induces his search for their stories
through dialogues with Mrs Rutherford and Christie, none of
which solve the mystery. The narrator's search for the essence of
Englishness also ends in the failure in which the initial project is
steeped. His one solid achievement is the building of the sea-wall
which should protect the values he seeks in the village.

Dabydeen engages in a complex of dialogues with Conrad,
Wilson Harris and V.S. Naipaul in charting the narrator's movement from engineering education by the good Professor Fenwick.
(Fenwick is the name of the protagonist of Harris' *The Secret Ladder*, also an engineer). Professor Fenwick acts as counter to the
corrupt Jack, who echoes Conrad's Kurtz in *Heart of Darkness* in
his mysterious excesses with black women. Jack is, of course, an
important character in Naipaul's *The Enigma of Arrival*, the embodiment of unvarying and timeless country virtues, as compared
to Dabydeen's Jack, who seems the embodiment of country vices.
The dog Jack is a witty invention, undercutting the seriousness of

the narrative by comic allusion to fellow dogs in British imperial writings, notably in Buchan's *Prester John*.[2]

Jack, despite the homely name, is the new hollow man, without Kurtz's imagination or bombast. Speaking in engineering terms, Mrs Rutherford observes that he went towards his desires in one straight line: though deviant in his tastes, certain in his aim. In Wilson Harris's *The Eye of the Scarecrow*, there is a similar reference to the engineer's absence of the erotic in the approach to the sexual act. The narrator tells us that he sent a grotesque woman to L his engineering friend, and when he asked L how he had made out with her "... he looked at me with his blank look as if he had not attempted to strip her at all, had been content merely to penetrate through everything, clothing, flesh, hair and gristle, with a blind and instinctive precision, a total acceptance of his responsible and her unalterable necessity, which made her naked compliance the most riddling factor of all."[3] Jack, like L, approached African women with a total absence of the erotic. Jack and his fellow expats sought domination rather than dialogue with Africa. For Mrs Rutherford, who has sought empathy and understanding, her experiences in Africa, "... made me know for the first time what we really are, outside of England and the decencies of the garden, the farm and the cottages."[4]

Mrs Rutherford and Jack represent two methods of relating to the Other: Jack through appetitive excess and violence; Mrs Rutherford by 'getting-under-the-skin' of the Other through empathy. She combines these sexual echoes in her advice to the narrator about the most effective way of approaching an English woman, and seeking the essence of Englishness:

> "Perhaps you can do it without Jack's nasty motives. Just the sheer thrill of nerves as you slide your hand up her thighs, the whiteness of it, the strange hungry flesh, the down of fine blond hair. And don't do it mechanically, don't gouge her flesh as if you were digging one of your canals. Soft, surpris-

ingly oblique touches, insinuating and playful. Isn't that the way to seek out England's story and make the connection you want?"[5]

This echoes one of Dabydeen's ideas, which he has repeated on radio programmes and elsewhere, namely, that sexual merging across racial and cultural boundaries is ultimately the most efficacious means of overcoming differences and hostilities. Carnal knowledge of the Other is one means of overcoming cultural and historical ignorance: in the sexual act, differences of flesh, history, culture etc. dissolve and true knowing can begin.

The novel suggests that there are two methods of approaching the Other: the wooer's eroticism and the engineer's domination; feminine and masculine. If Kurtz and Jack represent the one approach, exploitation and control, Mrs Rutherford represents the wooer's insinuating eroticism. Christie suggests that she might have been involved with a number of lovers in the village, and, in her words, she was "no madonna" in Africa. The narrator rests uneasily between these two positions; as an engineer he is both attracted by the ineffability of the sea, and wishes to control it. The sea represents for him the welcome capacity to overcome fixity:

> I was seduced by its endless transformations, which promised me freedom from being fixed as an African, a West-Indian, a member of a particular nationality of a particular epoch. The stories of my personal life could easily be extinguished in its mass.[6]

But control of it symbolises a desire to assert his identity in the face of the seamlessness of reality. He is both drawn towards Mrs Rutherford and nauseated by her aged flesh.

Jack, in contrast, is the modern savage who has traduced and abused African patience and gentleness. If Kurtz, in the throes of alienation and nihilism, declared: "exterminate the brutes," Jack had a "bulldozer mentality": "He'd bulldoze them into submission with his superior money, superior skin colour, superior civilisation."[7]

Jack and Kurtz represent the extreme manifestations of the violence towards the Other which Emmanuel Levinas suggests in *Totality and Infinity* resides in the very interstices of Western thought. Levinas associates this violence with the Socratic tradition and its elevation of the primacy of the same: "This primacy of the same was Socrates's teaching: to receive nothing of the Other but what is in me, as though from all eternity I was in possession of what comes to me from outside – to receive nothing, or to be free."[8] Bludgeoning the Other with the "light of theory" and the "enlightenment of knowledge" can lead ultimately, in the very formulation of these notions, to the atavism of Kurtz and Jack.

Mrs Rutherford suggests that patient allusiveness is the most effective method of approaching the Other. Unlike Kurtz's 'Intended' in *Heart of Darkness* Mrs Rutherford has lost any glittering illusions about European activities in Africa. She echoes another of Conrad's themes: the darkness which Europeans bring to Africa. In Conrad's book it is clearly the darkness which Kurtz brings to Africa, modern bourgeois man's sense of the absence of a ruling European morality, and the possibilities for what Michael Foucault terms the darkness of the unthought, which dominate the novel. The popular reading of the novel as Kurtz's corruption by the perversions of the bush fall for Conrad's gesture towards, and play with, the European notion of 'darkest Africa'.

If Conrad's Marlow employs various masks of irony and farce to hide the appalling reality of colonial Africa, Mrs Rutherford uses her masks to remind herself of the awful reality of Africans' lives, to strip herself of any illusions. The narrator's notion that her masks represented "sad symbols of Jack's conquest, abuse and abandonment of her," introduces an interpretation of her story which makes a parallel between hers and the African condition. The invitation to see the pitiableness of her condition as represented in the masks she calls her "evil children" is perhaps one we ought to resist so early in the narrative. This is the narrator's viewpoint and we ought perhaps to consider that this view is only one perspective in the novel and resist this premature closure of interpretation around Mrs Rutherford's situation.

The narrator engages in a search for the human story of the village through an exploration of the relationship between Mrs Rutherford, Jack and other eccentrics in it. A meeting with Curtis will, he believes, lead him to the mystery of Jack. The mystery of England is also involved in this search:

> The mystery of Jack would at least give me *something* to engage with until my time came to return to Guyana. Perhaps that was all that was left of England – a faint sense of mystery, enough to twitch your nose; a damp and musty smell, like the books lining the shelves of Mrs Rutherford's cottage. The books told fresh, triumphant stories about the latest deeds of Empire. They spoke with assurance about discoveries in science and manufacturing, about geographical explorations, about the moral conquest of dark and heathen minds. They were certain of the destiny of the English race. But, as Christie rightly said, the Empire had ended and what was left was a palsied decay . . .[9]

The search for Englishness is connected with the narrator's search for his own colonial roots, and is as illusive. Naipaul's travels in *The Enigma of Arrival* are connected with a search for his vocation as a writer. His walk in the English countryside parallels his various travels, his different arrivals, and he seeks to place them in a coherence which can be represented in writing. Dabydeen's narrator walks in a Sussex village in search of the mystery of the English, shadowing his search for the story of his colonial roots. As in Naipaul's case the journey in the metropolitan centre involves a symbolic search for colonial origins. In the narrator's case this also involves an attempt to experiment with the centre as Other, to make England and the English the Other. Of the English the narrator notes: "They assessed me by my surface, my skin colour and the quality of my suit, but although they were hidden from me I knew what they looked like inside ... such knowledge however gave me no power over them, as Mrs Rutherford had hoped."[10] On the contrary it is he who remains the outsider whom the villagers can fixate through their carapace of colonial ideology:

> They saw on the surface of my face the testimony of the masks, and they hid or kept to themselves, partly out of fright, partly out of realisation that I was so different from them that I might as well be invisible. After a while, when they got over the shock of my appearance, they looked hard at me and quite possibly saw nothing.[11]

In the introduction to *Hogarth's Blacks* Dabydeen states that Blacks were already part of the English world centuries ago. Used in illustrations, they were a familiar part of the English scene. The Black engineer's search for Englishness represents the attempt by the colonial to interrogate the culture which has determined his invisibility. Prospero renders Caliban invisible by proclaiming himself Caliban's alter ego: Caliban is *his* "thing of darkness", *his* Other, not an other in his own right, just as Blacks were regarded as English differences not differences in their own right. Their ubiquitous presence on English signboards, prints and paintings, to which Dabydeen attests, suggests that Blacks were for centuries part of an English world they were nonetheless not allowed to interrogate. They were used as illustrations, thus manifesting their invisibility, and abused as agents of degradation, thus declaring their difference. Dabydeen's novel is an attempt to turn the spotlight on that which would render him invisible by absorbing his blackness and proclaiming in effect: "this Black I acknowledge mine."

A theme which courses through the narrative is the contrast between the surface tranquillity and order of the village and the wildness and perturbation hidden beneath, a theme to which Mrs Rutherford constantly returns. She is constantly criticising the narrator's naiveté in his view of England which has been created by the gentle Professor Fenwick. Fenwick represents one colonial face of England. Jack is the contrast; the deviousness and sexual excess beneath the civilized demeanour. Perhaps theirs are both faces of England. Being English is therefore a complex of things: " ... a virus which we pass among ourselves and become immune to."[12] The "English sickness" is a colonial disease which is passed onto the unsuspecting colonized. But colonialism is also Professor Fenwick, gentleness and modesty, the domination of nature through patient science.

The theme of dominance recurs throughout the narrative. Dominance is associated with civilization. In Conrad's story London too has been one of the dark places of the world, but Marlow refers to a London whose darkness has been silted and covered by civilization. Dabydeen's narrator encounters a land, in England, whose darkness has been etiolated by civilization, a darkness to which Mrs Rutherford points him, being part of it herself in her connection with the obscure and perverse Jack and also as someone truly aware of the dark excesses of English history with which she has acquainted her pupils in Africa. England has also been dominated and quelled in "a sense of the law of the land."[13] Unlike the other nearby villages which have been invaded by the middle class, Dunsmere's history of domination and conquest has been preserved and is threatened only by the sea, a threat which the Black engineer is engaged in meeting.

The narrator is a professional, with a passion for conquering nature, from a culture nominally primitive and irrational. His belief in the values of engineering is countered by Mrs Rutherford's

belief in her African masks and her attribution of animist tenden-
cies to him, which challenges his self-image. Here there is a connection with Wilson Harris's tale of science and magic in which
many of his protagonists are engineers or surveyors engaged in
scientific projects, whose encounters with the ineffable lead to
personal reassessment. In *The Secret Ladder*, Fenwick's encounter
with Poseidon, an ancient Black leader, results in a reconsidera-
tion of his life and outlook. In Dabydeen's novel the narrator's encounter with the contradictions and darknesses of England and
Englishness confounds his engineer's sense of knowledge and
leads to the occasional outburst of angst against Mrs Rutherford.

The search for Englishness ends in irresolution. Nor has the
narrator at the end of the novel discovered more of Curtis or Jack,
although he does learn through some newspaper cuttings of Mrs
Rutherford that Jack and Curtis, as husband and probable lover,
were possibly involved in some "seedy narrative of adultery ..."
Curtis's grand scheme for protecting the village was ultimately
opposed by the villagers, and so his story ended in "civic squab-
bles." This is all England seems to offer him. The narrator's
search ends in failure because he is everywhere surrounded by
the English who are to be found everywhere and nowhere. It is
Mrs Rutherford, both English, and as it were not English, who is
not capable of perceiving the peculiarity of Englishness, since her
character and experiences make her more capable of the kind of
metamorphoses necessary to become both self and other. She can
be both African and English out of a capacity for empathy
whereas the narrator in a sense represents an international modern figure, the self-made professional who seeks to banish all
traces of darkness, the irrational, the Other, in the act of self-
creation.

The novel is a complex variation of echoing and allusive
themes, sometimes beckoning to each other, sometimes embrac-
ing, drawing the reader into their fine web. If Conrad's *Heart of
Darkness* interrogates European values at one of its 'outposts of

progress' in Africa, David Dabydeen's novel investigates the colonial centre, seeking its darkness within its very borders.

Notes

1   David Dabydeen, *Disappearance* (London: Secker & Warburg, 1993), pp. 38-39. All further references to the novel are to this edition.

2   Dabydeen has written about the imperial dog in several essays. His analysis of John Buchan's *Prester John* begins: "One can reduce Buchan's tale to its absurd essentials by saying it is a story about a Britisher and his dog who between them put down a great native uprising in Africa" (D Dabydeen and N Wilson-Tagoe, *A Reader's Guide to West Indian and Black British Literature* [Hansib, 1988], pp.111 ff).

3   Wilson Harris, *The Eye of the Scarecrow* (London: Faber, 1965), p. 50.

4   *Disappearance*, p. 77.

5   Op. cit. p. 76.

6   Op. cit. p. 132.

7   Op. cit. p. 76.

8   Emmanuel Levinas, *Totality and Infinity* (Amsterdam: Martin Nijoff Publishers, 1979), p. 43.

9   *Disappearance*, p. 133.

10 Op. cit. pp. 130-131.

11 Ibid.

12 Op. cit. p. 95.

13 Op. cit. pp. 92-93.

CHAPTER VII

'SELF-CONSCIOUSLY POST-COLONIAL':
THE FICTION OF DAVID DABYDEEN

MARK McWATT

I have chosen to write on the novels of David Dabydeen because
it can be argued that postcolonial theory and West Indian Literature come into close identification in his fiction. This is because
Dabydeen is an author who, perhaps because he is also an academic lecturing on literature in a university, is self-consciously
aware of the latest trends in contemporary literary theory and
seems to have in mind the arguments and shibboleths of this
theory as he constructs his fiction. Prominently identifiable
among the fictional techniques of this author are some of the classical counter-discursive strategies associated with post-colonial
theory.[1] This is true of Dabydeen's first novel, *The Intended*,[2] but
perhaps ever more so of his recently published second novel, *Disappearance*,[3] of which the title itself has a kind of theoretical
resonance.

In the brief span of this essay I set out to accomplish two
things: to establish the self-conscious operation of postcolonial
counter-discursive techniques in the novels by discussing inci-
dents and passages in the texts; and to consider briefly the effect
of the author's self-conscious manipulation of the 'fiction' to accommodate the requirements of the theoretical positions he is exploring. With reference to the latter task I intend a distinction
between 'deliberate' and 'self-conscious'; I accept that counter-

discursive strategies within a post-colonial text can be either deliberate, on the part of the author, or an unconscious feature of
discourse, given that fiction cannot, in any real sense, exist apart
from ideology.[4]

The most obvious counter-discursive strategy employed by
Dabydeen in *The Intended* is what Helen Tiffin has called
"canonical counter-discourse",[5] which involves "writing back" to
a text that would therefore have helped to shape the values and
the consciousness of postcolonial peoples. In the Dabydeen novel
the canonical text is Conrad's *Heart of Darkness*, long identified
as a favourite target of postcolonial writers.[6] The very title of
Dabydeen's novel conjures up Kurtz's fiancée – referred to as his
"intended" – and re-inscribes that particular complex of futility
and passionate misapprehension at the heart of the later novel,
where it is nevertheless subverted by the reader's uncertainty
about whether the "intended" is the narrator, his girlfriend or
perhaps the novel itself. Apart from the disruptive intertextuality
of the reference, "The Intended" could also be a sly and
deliberate assertion of authorial 'intention' with regard to the use
of counter-discursive strategies.

The centrality of the Conrad novel to Dabydeen's counter-discourse is indicated by the fact that the unnamed narrator is
studying it for his A-level Literature exam. The counter-discursive critique of the novel, however, does not come from the aca-
demically brilliant narrator, but rather from his friend Joseph, an
illiterate black rasta youth. Here is a passage that follows a request from Joseph that the narrator reread the "bit about them
[the blacks] lying under the trees dying":

> I flicked through, found the passage and read it aloud to
> him. "That's part of the theme of suffering and redemption
> which lies at the core of the novel's concern", I stated co-
> gently and intelligently, putting the book down.

"No, it ain't, is about colours. You been saying is a novel
'bout the fall of man, but is really 'bout a dream. Beneath
the surface is the dream. The white light of England and the
Thames is the white sun over the Congo that can't mix with
the green of the bush and the black skin of the people. All
the colours struggling to curve against each other like rainbow, but instead the white light want to blot out the black
and the green and reduce the world to one blinding colour."
(p.98)

Not only does Joseph's reading illuminate *Heart of Darkness*
with its freshness and passion, but it also counters the narrator's
received critical wisdom as well as denying the closure implicit in
his words: "... I stated cogently and intelligently, putting the book
down." It is Joseph who reopens the dialogue between text and
reader in a way which startles the narrator by interrogating his
critical learning, supplying instead a visionary, postcolonial reading of the novel's meaning. The fact that such a reading is available to the illiterate Joseph, and not to the narrator is a further
counter-discursive ploy, countering the assumed marginality of
the black, illiterate 'other'. Not only is Joseph able to discern the
imperial function in the discourse of the centre, but he expresses
a desire to appropriate that discourse and subvert it with his own
vision: he wants to make a film of *Heart of Darkness;* the fact that
he never does so is a failure of means, rather than perception.[7]

Joseph's rainbow reading of the colours in *Heart of Darkness*
might suggest the notion, dear to postcolonial theory, of
syncreticity – a vision of culture based upon the complexity and
richness of a post-colonial world composed of diverse elements;
in another passage he has Joseph comment with similar counter-
discursive cogency on the language and music of Milton's
'Lycidas' – again making the point of that poem's 'availability' to
the marginal spirit, uninscribed with the values of the imperial
text. But as he continues his commentary it becomes clear that
Joseph is haunted by a vision of purity:

"Lycidas dead and gone to a world where nowaday-things don't matter nothing, like white people against black people, like thieving and hustling and pimping and rioting, like slavery and all that kind of history. The man turn pure spirit, pure like flowing water, that's why it's all water talk, the theme thing is water. His body bathe and the spirit come out clean-clean and clear – not white or black, but clear. All of we is music, all of we is clear underneath, inside . . ." (pp.147-8)

The emphasis on purity and unity here sounds very much like a retreat from the earlier hint of syncreticity to a universalist and essentialist paradigm. In fact Joseph's discourse, though illuminating at points, becomes more rambling as he sinks under the weight of his own crucial inadequacies and of his horror at the filth of his world as he becomes a cameraman for Patel, shooting pornographic movies: "Nasty, a lot of nastiness they're up to ... Fed up with filth. Sex. Sex. Filth . . ." (p.234)

These words become his own equivalent of Kurtz's "The horror", and he ends his life by setting himself afire. It is clear that Joseph's role in the novel as postcolonial critic is a partial one; the author's self-conscious engagement with the world of theory ensures this. But, with the author as manipulator, Joseph's death itself becomes a statement within the novel's counter discourse. His final role as a black Kurtz from the margins finding his heart of (sexual) darkness at the imperial centre questions the values of the imperial text and subverts the perception of these as axiomatic. The dominant discourse is destabilized by the interposition of a marginal character like Joseph, invested, as it were, with canonical authority through his partial equation with Kurtz.

Elsewhere in the novel is subverted one of the more important motifs of the imperial text: the journey from the centre to the margins of Empire, a paradigm that encompasses journeys of discovery, of conquest, of settlement. *Heart of Darkness* is subjected to further counter-discursive strategy as the journey up the Congo is trivialized to a fairground ride. The summer job of the narrator and his friend Shaz is to operate the 'World Cruise' ride at the Battersea Fun Fair, where small boats take the riders through a dark tunnel, the walls of which have been painted with scenes from several countries – taken alphabetically, from Austria to Zanzibar. The alphabet of countries pokes fun not only at the implied completeness of the knowledge and vision available from the imperial centre, but it also identifies the far-flung margins of the world with the English alphabet, with the imperial language as shaping and containing vessel. The scenes depicting countries of the postcolonial world are, predictably, crudely stereotypical; "the men in Timbuktu wore necklaces made out of the teeth of animals and each had a bone running through his nostrils. A black woman with full breasts and gleaming thighs carried a pot on her head. Another sat on a donkey so oddly – her buttocks merged into its flank – that it seemed she was having some kind of bizarre sex with it." (p.78)

The grandiose design of the 'World Cruise' is further undercut by the motives of many of the patrons who pay for the ride; not at all interested in the countries depicted on the walls of the tunnel – nor in the imperial perspective those scenes might have been intended to reinforce – they seek the boat-ride into the heart of a little darkness in order to fornicate in relative privacy; the narrator says:

> On some mornings I would collect an assortment of underclothing, male and female, abandoned between Fiji and Timbuktu, two minutes into the ride and two minutes from the exit. (p.77)

The comic crudeness of this kind of counter-discourse clearly indicates the bias of the postcolonial perspective at this point, but Dabydeen's political and theoretical correctness extends to the deliberate subversion of that very bias, as the narrator himself is made to look crudely ridiculous standing in the bow of his little boat "torch in one hand, spiked aluminium rod like a fearsome weapon in the other", retrieving underwear (the residue of imperial adventure?) from the far countries of empire. He also has the task of erasing the sexual graffiti from the naked bodies of the African tribesmen. The narrator is made to succumb to the essentialist concept of pride in national identity as he yearns for painted scenes of oil-wells, libraries and airports to replace the naked men and women depicting African countries. Hence Dabydeen has succeeded in devising textual strategies which, in the language of Wilson Harris, "consume their own biases"[8], suggesting the mutual embrace of oppressor and oppressed in a joint postcolonial project to transcend the fixed categories of history.

The already-mentioned suggestiveness of the title "The Intended" becomes resonant at the end of the novel, where the narrator's white girlfriend is about to leave for Australia, leaving the black narrator to travel further into the centre as he prepares to go to Oxford University. Which of them is the adventurer into the heart of darkness? The author knowingly has the girlfriend say to the narrator: "I can't send you there (Oxford) looking like something from the Congo ..." The many reversals and ironic reinscriptions of signs and suggestions so familiar within the imperial, canonical text create an eloquent uncertainty that becomes a very effective counter-discursive strategy at this point.

In Dabydeen's second novel, *Disappearance*, the narrator is an Afro-Guyanese engineer who find himself, as protégé of an English professor, supervising an engineering project aimed at saving a village on the cliffs of Kent from falling into the sea. The English professor is called Fenwick, a name which recalls Wilson Harris's *The Secret Ladder*, but the suggestion of intertextuality is more problematic here than in *The Intended*; in the first place the Harris novel occupies a very different position with regard to the imperial canon to that of *Heart of Darkness*; also, the name

Fenwick is the only reference to the text of the Harris novel – unless you include a teasing epigraph, one of several. In fact another such epigraph is from Conrad (though listed as a quote from T S Eliot) – "Mistah Kurtz – he dead" – and indeed it is *Heart of Darkness* more than any other text that resonates in the background of this novel as well.

The deliberate and self-conscious literary and theoretical games being played by the author in this novel surpass those of *The Intended*. The title suggests Derrida's notion of writing as "the disappearance of natural presence", and various aspects of that notion haunt the narrator throughout. Near the beginning, as he moves into the house of Mrs Rutherford where he is to board for the duration of the cliff-saving project, he contemplates the books on her shelf and the inscription therein, savouring, as it were, the Derridan "traces" of presence:

> Books that bore curious inscriptions in faded ink ... *Ex Libris Joseph Countryman Esq. Dominus Illuminatio Mea.* Others were more personal, making me feel intrusive and uncomfortable when I read them because I was from the future they could not envisage, a future which could well have brought terrors and disappointments to their evolving lives, a future which ruptured the innocence of the moment. *For Albert on being sixteen. May God keep you steadfast in your studies and may you prosper in His Grace and Wisdom. Your Loving Father; Dearest Annie, each word in this book tells your life and mine. Love John.* (p.9)

The first inscription (the motto of Oxford University) is curiously intertextual when we realize that Joseph Countryman is the name of the illiterate rasta youth in *The Intended;* to associate him in this way with text is to reject Eurocentric ideas of the value of text and to question as well the suggestion that Eurocentric notions of individual time and place can be transformed into objective historical narrative. Dabydeen follows the passage above with a postcolonial counter-discursive strategy aimed precisely at "rupturing the innocence of the moment":

> How was the father to know that Albert would indeed go on to become Professor of Classics at Oxford, Jack the Ripper's pimp or a leader of the Cato Street Conspiracy? And Annie, Dearest Annie, with apple-juice breasts that men gurgled and choked on, marble thighs that made men slip and break their necks; Annie who may have married John and lived in a farmhouse... Annie who, burdened with John's molestations and fetishes, perhaps absconded with an early Feminist and wrote treatises against Royalty, Episcopacy, the Judiciary and other phallocentric institutions. I held the book guiltily and excitedly as though I were a peeping Tom... (p.9)

Manipulated by the postcolonial awareness of the author, the narrator is made to stand counter to text, insinuating into its narrative fastnesses the chaos of possibility, of counter discourse. Like the bookworm which tunnels through the pages, he is able to see through the text to the endboards that represent the coffin and death. He questions the textual logic of the individual vision or experience as history and therefore questions the power and authority of imperial universalist paradigms. The narrator's freedom to interrogate the power of text stems from a postcolonial understanding of his otherness:

> I could read their books... without anxiety about the strangeness of the world drawn by their words. All this because I had no sense of the past, no sense of ruptured innocence. (p.10)

There is no sense of ruptured innocence because on the one hand he feels no allegiance to Eurocentric values which need to be reasserted in the face of shattering realities like Nazism or the disappearance of Empire; and on the other hand no sense of national or traditional cultural purity pertaining to his native Guyana or Caribbean and into which he can retreat in safety to watch the world and its pain pass by. Both of these essentialist positions are rejected in a postcolonial stance which is further worked out in the novel in terms of the narrator's opposition to two other major characters.

Mrs Rutherford, his landlady, is the first of these. Having lived for years in Africa and brought home a number of African masks, she proceeds to educate the narrator about his African roots. She has rejected English imperial values along with her husband, whose sexual predations among the native women symbolized these values for her. She yearns for revenge on behalf of postcolonial peoples and thus curiously represents the abrogation of the universalist claims of the imperial centre in favour of nationalist liberation. She tries unsuccessfully to persuade the narrator to this position.

The other character is Christie, an Irish workman on the sea-defence project, a complex character who deserves greater discussion than can be afforded him here. In terms of the postcolonial themes of the novel Christie is another colonial lured to the imperial centre but incapable of belonging to it. He is defeated by the completeness and pervasiveness of the imperial system: "They have everything and they have the words and all" (p.162), he tells the narrator. He retreats into the stereotype of the Irishman for protection: "I joke, I grin, I talk in a bog accent... I believe in fairies. I've been playing Paddy so long I've forgotten what it feels like to be a man..." (p.164) and he urges the same solution on the narrator who is seeking to extract the story (history?) of the village: "I keep telling you, don't pry into this country. Keep to yourself. Act black and dumb. Get the banjo out. Sing like Al Jolson. Run the hundred metres at the Olympics. Do anything but don't enquire too deeply or you're done for." (p.167)

His advice is to accept the stereotypes of the dominant discourse, because you (he) will always be excluded from its 'truth'. In the end he becomes so enraged at the narrator's persistent refusal to take his advice that he explodes:

> "Of course there are no fucking leprechauns... What do you take the Irish for, a bunch of pissed primitives? ... Look what the English leprechauns have done for you: fancy clothes, fancy words and fancy science. You've disappeared up the English cunt without knowing it. Me, I hold on to something else, even if I invent it. Call it Irishness if you want, call it anything, but at least I don't get sucked in. I'm still here, prick and all ..." (p.168)

His is an essentialist solution, clinging to the life-raft of his Irishness. He becomes another version of Kurtz contemplating "the horror", of which his outburst is the equivalent. He has travelled from (European) periphery to centre and discovered the heart of darkness. So too, in a sense, has the narrator, but he, ever imbued with the postcolonial wisdom of his author can react differently by blaming it all on the perfidy of the imperial text. As he retreats from the house of the raving Christie, he looks back and places everything in proper postcolonial perspective:

> From a safe distance his cottage had the appearance of a picturesque shambles... It was the kind of dwelling you'd imagine a hermit to be inhabiting, in an English fairytale from one of my story-books. When I looked again I could see it for what it was – woodwormed, crippled with hatred, wanting to crash to the ground more catastrophically than the cliff's fall. (p.169)

By perceiving the text as flawed, he is able to resist textual illusion of romance in a way that Christie could not.

The location of postcolonial counter-discursive strategies in terms of fictional characters in this essay is an attempt to focus upon the merging of fiction and theory. The self-consciously post-colonial narrator presents a difficulty; as Norval Edwards says about the narrator in *The Intended:*

> ... The young narrator is often burdened with an explanatory power that surpasses his years... We are not allowed to figure [things] out. *(Caribbean Review of Books, p.10).*

The problem remains in *Disappearance*. Political and theoretical correctness robs the narrator of life, his 'presence' is attenuated, (he 'disappears' as it were) and although this in itself is for the purpose of making a theoretical point, is the point worth the loss? Perhaps it is preferable for the reader to apply the theory to the text, rather than have the text apply it to itself. Perhaps, too, this could be David Dabydeen's point: that there is little substance at the centre of the self-consciously post-colonial text – no story apart from the enactment of theoretical paradigms. While it is true that no text exists apart from ideology, it is harder to accept that ideology should be its *raison d'etre*. A novel like Wilson Harris's *The Four Banks of the River of Space*, which is just as ideologically committed and is a superb postcolonial text, remains more true to the imperatives of the narrative imagination than to textual politics or theory. *The Intended* is rescued by stories and by the cultural cross-fertilization of Guyana and London. In the later novel the narrator abandons Guyana as a narrative locus before the novel's halfway point; there are stories, but they exist in order to be contradicted and discredited later on. The denial of narrative satisfaction is a deliberate authorial intrusion, rather than the 'discovery' of the reader. Christie spells it out towards the end of the novel:

Pick whatever version of whatever story you prefer, it's all the same. You can't know anything in life for sure, you might as well make it up.(p.168)

All this constitutes marvellous literary gamesmanship, what with the narrative disappearing, as it were, up its own aporia, and it conscripts the reader as an accomplice to his own disappearance – if there is no 'truth' in the novel (except the endless restatement of the political correctness of postcolonial theory) then the reader is at least as diminished as the fiction.

Notes

1   The main outline of postcolonial Theory can be found in B Ashcroft et al, *The Empire Writes Back* (London: Routledge, 1989); but see also Helen Tiffin: 'Post Colonial Literatures and Counter-Discourse' in *Kunapipi* IX, 3, 1987, pp 17-34.

2   David Dabydeen, *The Intended* (London: Secker & Warburg), 1991.

3   David Dabydeen, *Disappearance* (London: Secker & Warburg), 1993.

4   For a discussion of the importance of the author's awareness or otherwise of the counter-discursive techniques in his fiction, see *The Empire Writes Back, op. cit.*

5   *Kunapipi*, IX, 3, 1987 p 22.

6   See Chinua Achebe, 'An Image of Africa' in *Research in African Literatures*, 9, I (1978) pp 1-15; V S Naipaul's 'Conrad's Darkness' in *The Return of Eva Peron with The Killings in Trinidad* (London: Deutsch, 1980), pp. 207-228; and Wilson Harris, 'The Frontier on which *Heart of Darkness* Stands' in *Explorations* (Denmark: Dangaroo Press, 1981), pp. 134-141.

7   Joseph's reading of *Heart of Darkness* has been previously discussed by Norval Edwards in a review of *The Intended* in *Caribbean Review of Books*, 4, May 1992. Edwards discussion makes several of the points made here.

8   Wilson Harris, 'Adversarial Contexts and Creativity', in *New Left Review*, 154 (Nov-Dec 1985), p 127.

CHAPTER VIII

A LABYRINTHINE ODYSSEY:
PSYCHIC DIVISION IN THE WRITINGS
OF DAVID DABYDEEN

MARIO RELICH

Time the destroyer is time the preserver
Like the river with its cargo of dead negroes, cows
and chicken coops,
The bitter apple and the bite in the apple
['The Dry Salvages' *(Four Quartets)* by T S Eliot]

That people with a long history at the receiving end of exploitative
colonialism, particularly the West Indians, are torn between the
cultures and values they could salvage from their ancestors,
whether slaves or indentured workers, and that of metropolitan
cultures and values borrowed from the colonial exploiters is now
almost commonplace. The phenomenon needed, however, to be
articulated in psychological and sociological terms by cultural
critics such as Frantz Fanon and, more recently, Edward Said.
Such a rupture in the colonized undoubtedly led to much personal
unhappiness, and even irreconcilable conflict, within many an
individual psyche. In the form of "creative schizophrenia", as
Michael Gilkes put it,[1] however, it has released the writerly
energies of such diverse West Indian novelists and poets as Derek
Walcott, Wilson Harris, and George Lamming, to name only a few
of the most distinguished.

My aim here is to focus on David Dabydeen as a writer who is particularly intent in finding objective equivalents for dramatizing a conflict which is essentially *inner*.[2] To put it another way, both in his poetry and in his fiction Dabydeen explores the complexities of psychic division. He begins to do so in his two books of poems, *Slave Song* (1984) and *Coolie Odyssey* (1988), but does so most comprehensively in *The Intended* (1991), his first novel.

Psychic division at its most brutal, originating in the murky depths of sexual desire, permeates every poem in *Slave Song*. The poems, all in creole, tend to be anguished monologues from Guyanese canecutters of East Indian descent. The drudgery and sheer suffering of their lives are compensated for (rather inadequately of course) in sexual fantasies. At the bottom of these sexual fantasies, however, are psychic divisions. In 'The Canecutters' Song', for example, the focus of lustful fantasy is a white woman. Yet there is a kind of purity in their frustrated desires, which is indicated in their resort to Hindu incantations, as in the following lines:

O Shanti! Shanti! Shanti!
Wash dis dutty-skin in yu dew
Wipe am clean on yu saaf white petal!
O Shanti! Shanti! Shanti! —
So me spirit call, so e halla foh yu[3]

The sublimation of their desires barely hides what they really want, thereby making the poem very close to ironic.

Dabydeen's copious notes to this poem, as well as all the others, suggest further dimensions to psychic division. The notes, together with his impassioned introductory essay on the stunted lives of the cane-cutters, form an integral part of the *experience* of reading *Slave Song*, much as Eliot's notes are indispensable to *The Waste Land*. The same can be said of the discussion in the same essay of dialect: "It's hard to put two words together in Creole without swearing."[4] Like *The Waste Land*, in short, *Slave*

Song is not a text of poetry with editorial notes, but a text made up of poetry and prose. Dabydeen's notes, moreover, rival Eliot's in their possum-like playfulness. He tells us about the woman in 'The Canecutters' Song', for instance, that "She wants to be degraded secretly (the long lace frock is temptingly rich, and it hangs loose, suggestively; also the chaos of her hair), to be possessed and mutilated in the mud" and that "The tragedy is as much hers for her desires too are prevented by social barriers".[5] This commentary, however, is rather misleading, not least because the poem itself never leaves the consciousness of the cane-cutters. The observations about the white woman's desires read like an unwarranted interpolation, a highly ironic one because the fantasies are now those of the poet rather than those of the cane-cutters. The poet thereby draws attention to his own alienation and psychic divisions, and in a complex, ironic manner that seems to be missed in an otherwise authoritative essay on Dabydeen's poems by Benita Parry, precisely because she foregrounds the poems and neglects the commentary.[6] Neither the poem, nor the annotations to it, however, can capture the full dramatic potential of the scene. Only reading *both* poem and annotation can do that. *Slave Song*, in short, reveals a violent "dissociation of sensibility" within the poet's own psyche, and one that Eliot (who coined the phrase) as author of the 'Sweeney' poems, would have recognized.

The final poem in *Slave Song*, 'Two Cultures', suggests the next step in Dabydeen's exploration of psychic divisions. The speaker here is an old man, and the situation, according to the notes, "a common one in Guyana." A father, in short, puts a young Guyanese firmly in his place, even though the latter has just re-turned in triumph from England. After a long diatribe, he ends with the following shattering diminishment:

So yu tink yu can come hey an play big-shat,
Fill we eye wid cigarette, iceapple an all dat?

> Aweh po country people but aweh ga pride;
> Jess touch me gyal-pickni, me go buss yu back-side.[7]

The poems in *Coolie Odyssey,* however, are precisely about such a 'prodigal son' figure. They reveal how he is a rather more complex person than the old father of 'Two Cultures' is capable of assuming, yet also prey to deep psychic divisions.

The long title-poem which opens *Coolie Odyssey* describes how the poet, something of an exile, is affected by psychic divisions *within* English literary culture. This is why the opening lines, which sardonically begin with "Now that peasantry is in vogue", allude to English poets considered 'provincial', but also highly fashionable. Lines like "Poetry from peat bogs" and "People strain for the old folk's fatal gobs/ Coughed up in grates North or North East"[8] irresistibly remind one of poets like Seamus Heaney and Tony Harrison. Such poets, who celebrate local communities, or mourn their passing, but in language sophisticated or 'street-wise' enough to please metropolitan readers (particularly critics) were highlighted in the very influential *Penguin Book of Contemporary British Poetry* (1982), which was edited by Blake Morrison and Andrew Motion. It reveals a kind of literary and cultural context within which the Guyanese poet feels very uneasy, and prone to satirical shafts, though also paradoxically knowing exactly how to operate within it. That is why he describes his verse as "Poems that scrape bone and bowl/In English basements far from home" and addressed "To congregations of the educated/Sipping wine, attentive between courses–."[9] The Preface to the volume describes the poem as "offering glimpses into an odyssey, not a chronicle of threaded events."[10] But the odyssey is a poignant, circular one, for at the bleak centre of the poem is a funeral missed, and a visit to a village cemetery: "... this library of graves,/this small clearing of scrubland."[11] The poet can only return to Britain, the land of his metropolitan audience. Odysseus at least could return to his faithful Penelope.

Where *Coolie Odyssey* significantly differs from *Slave Song* is that the poems it contains are much more direct about dealing with psychic divisions suffered by the poet himself. He focuses on himself, and how he, as a Guyanese, and one descended from Hindu Indians, has turned into a British writer. Linton Kwesi Johnson has perhaps best defined Dabydeen's achievement in *Coolie Odyssey*:

> Throughout these poems we find a confluence of past and present, the personal and the historical which are seemingly effortlessly intertwined in memories of "back-home". His voice is the cool, reflective one of distance and detachment, the voice of the exile whose return is a journey back in time.[12]

One poem, 'London Taxi Driver', however, returns to the territory of *Slave Song*, even if in a rather more complex manner.

It describes a driver, West Indian and of Hindu descent, full of self-loathing expressed as violent misogyny. His bitter observations are 'reported' to the reader by an urbane passenger who is not likely to be other than the poet himself. It becomes only deceptively 'cool' and 'reflective' particularly as the driver may be a kind of Mr Hyde to the poet's Dr Jekyll. Such a reading undermines the gentility of the poetic voice observing this particular taxi driver. Here is the conclusion, voiced by the poet-passenger:

> Now he knows more the drama of amber, red and green,
> Mutinies against double-yellow lines,
> His aggression is horned like ancient clarions,
> He grunts rebellion
> In back seat discount sex
> With the night's last whore.[13]

If in *Coolie Odyssey* Dabydeen finds his voice as 'exile', even therapeutically so, in a poem like 'London Taxi Driver' it is in a very ambivalent manner. In *The Intended* the author adopts a semi-autobiographical prose form, the 'bildungsroman', or 'apprenticeship novel', and succeeds in exploring his own psychic divisions in a different, more open-ended manner than his two volumes of poetry. The 'bildungsroman' can be defined as a novel, usually with a first-person narrator, which focuses on the process of growing up, and the ways in which "child is father to the man", especially if that child becomes a writer. *The Intended*, to some extent, subverts this kind of novel, which is so prominent in the European tradition, just as the poems in *Slave Song* subvert the dramatic monologue. Two of the most famous novels in this genre in English are Dickens's *Great Expectations* and Joyce's *Portrait of the Artist as a Young Man.* In terms of narrative technique, one striking aspect of both is that the narrators, Pip in one case, and Stephen Dedalus in the other, provide a double perspective on their experiences. In both cases, though the narrator is a single person, his perspective is sometimes that of the older person who has 'written' the narrative, and sometimes, indeed very intensely so, that of the child or young man experiencing the vicissitudes of life in a completely direct manner. Dabydeen, however, provides a *triple* perspective, for his unnamed young man makes a sharp distinction between his experiences as a child in what was then British Guiana, and as a teenager living in the Balham district of London.

The third perspective comes from his vantage point as a university student on a scholarship in Oxford.

This kind of triple perspective is not unprecedented, the most famous example being perhaps Charlotte Bronte's *Jane Eyre,* where Jane's childhood is clearly distinguished from her experiences as a governess working for Rochester, but her vantage point is that of the woman who has already 'tamed' him. In both *Jane Eyre* and *The Intended*, in other words, the *rupture* between childhood and adolescence is rather more important than in the aforementioned novels of Dickens and Joyce.

In a sense, however, and here I am talking about narrative technique, Dabydeen goes even further than Bronte. This is because the childhood experiences are not described chronologically, as is the case not only in Bronte, but Dickens and Joyce as well. Rather, the childhood recollections tend to disrupt the narrative of adolescent experiences in *The Intended*, often unexpectedly.

One such early 'flashback' occurs when the narrator, who has been abandoned by his Guyanese father in Britain, walks alone, provoked by his treatment at the hands of his friend's mother:

> I walked down Bedford Hill feeling sorry for myself, wishing I had a family to go home to. Nasim's mother was like my grandmother who waited by the roadside and when I stepped off the bus at Albion village would take my hand tightly in hers and lead me across the dam to a drum of water in the yard. She took my bag upstairs and returned with a cotton vest, a powder tin and towel. Then she unbuttoned my shirt and trousers, folded them neatly to one side, and poured water over me, rubbing in soap and washing it away, all the time interrogating me about how my mother was doing, how my sisters, if the house roof repair yet, how my father treating all of we, if he does still drink rum and beat, if my mother is saving up she money. I spluttered out answers as best I could, the soapy water flowing down my face, making me squeeze my eyes or spit whenever I answered a question and the water ran into my mouth. She dried me vigorously, raised my arms and splashed powder everywhere.[14]

The recollection is sensuously vivid, and thereby seems worlds away from the narrator's bleak description of his walking "down Bedford Hill". In fact, temporarily and spatially, his recollection is not only worlds away, but totally vanished into the past; moreover, it is psychologically right, for what could be more natural than remembering a moment of warmth, and so vividly that it is at least 'present' to the reader, in the midst of chilly solitude? The flashback, moreover, is no temporary one, but goes on for pages and actually concludes the first of the novel's four parts. The rupture between past and present is reflected in the way Dabydeen's language slips from adult standard English to childhood's creole. Such slippages occur throughout the narrative and are beautifully unobtrusive at times, drawing the reader effortlessly and cunningly into the text. The 'confusion' of verb tenses within the creole language further complicates the time-scheme of the novel as well as conveying a sense of the narrator's psychic disorientation.

The contrast between the narrator's past life in Guyana, and his very recent life in Balham, is not so much that as a child he was 'at home' and in Balham an 'immigrant' struggling to survive in the host society. What really counts is that the *texture* of life in Guyana is radically different, and the people described almost seem denizens of another dimension. One example shows how the narrator's memories of his life in Guyana take on a 'heroic' quality. In the following extract, he recollects a figure who became larger than life:

> Peter's father, a small-boned insignificant peasant who spent all his life in a cow pasture or paddy field, took on legendary proportions, transformed into the hero and villain, pioneer, pilot, politician, technician, saviour and beast; those hardly noticing him now began to dream about him. It was Auntie Pakul, the night before a fire mysteriously gutted her house, destroying all the dollar notes and melting the gold she had saved up over the years in a rice-sack hidden under a loose floorboard, who disclosed to my grandmother that she had dreamt Peter's father was metamorphosed into a firefly, flapping giant wings, which when outspread, cast a black shadow over the earth, and rubbing his feet together could create bolts of lightening — an image that could have

come straight out of Shaz's record sleeves, except that it was
more imaginative in conception ... (p.56)

The narrator here alludes to his life in Britain only briefly, but
tellingly in the observation about his friend Shaz's record sleeves.
The reason for doing so becomes clear when the reader recalls
that this is what the narrator said about Shaz in the opening pages
of the novel:

> He amassed a collection of rock LPs and was fascinated by
> the surrealistic cover designs, splashes of electronically
> processed colours forming weird patterns and shapes: the
> contours of breast and other half-glimpsed parts of the fe-
> male body, futuristic animals in a dreamy landscape, huge
> boulders breaking and crashing into a river of molten ice,
> and his favourite of all – a huge black creature, half-man,
> half-bird, squatting over a nest of white eggs, enveloping
> them protectively in its broad wings, whilst from the edge of
> the frame the sinister barrel of a gun protruded. (p.4)

Shaz, unlike the narrator, however, never becomes a writer, or
artist of any kind. The extract where the record sleeves are referred to again, only this time in relation to Auntie Pakul's imagination, subtly suggests why. In the Guyana (or British Guiana)
where the narrator grew up, though hard drinking was common,
there was no need for synthetic ways of stimulating the imagination.

Although other factors also operate in the narrator's eventual
decision to become a writer, it is his storehouse of memories
which makes for the decisive factor. This is made abundantly
clear in two recollections of Richilo. In the first, the narrator dis-
cusses with the worldly and uncomprehending Shaz his reasons
for gravitating towards a writing career, when he suddenly remembers Richilo:

'It will take twenty years of hard work and studying; why don't you just do a few exams and get a job with lots of money?' Shaz wanted to know. 'Because that is the way I am,' I told him, mysteriously, 'money's not everything,' and as soon as I spoke the words the memory of a drunken Richilo sliding about in the mud, like a new calf unsteady on its legs, returned. (pp.113-14)

Richilo, in fact, comes to represent for the narrator a kind of role-model, which in the context of his own life in Britain meant that he would have to become a writer. The key passage which implies this is the following:

She boxed my ears, sent me downstairs, where I mooned among the sheep grazing in the yard, waiting to be driven into the pen. I hated the smell of sheep, they dropped black dung everywhere which oozed between my toes. Even when I washed my feet the smell remained. I hated the nastiness of the whole village. I hated my grandmother. Richilo was right to curse her, calling her a tar-baby, a low-caste, louse-ridden, yam-headed, dog-eared, hungry-belly, black-skinned, buck-toothed whore, more sour-mouthed than tamarind, more hard-hearted than turtle shell, more slimy than fish-guts, stinkier than latrine, more pissy than monsoon, more . . . he took one last swig of rum and running out of images collapsed on his rice-sack bed. I hid under the bed-sheet, trembling with fear yet aroused by his power of speech. I wished I could describe things like Richilo. (pp.227-28)

Later in the same passage, the narrator observes: "I was confident that when I grew up I would be as clever as Richilo in seeing things and using words" (p.228). Richilo here may be squalid, but he is squalid in the grand manner, and his capacity to curse ironically indicates his creativity. Above all, despite his poverty, and his drink problem, there is a heroic quality to his escapades, part and parcel of his eloquence. The significance of remembering Richilo for the narrator is that Richilo, more than anyone else in the past, stimulates him to become a writer. His creative energies are released, in fact, by his acceptance of his remembered life in Guyana, when he spoke mainly in creole, and was at the receiving end of the whiplash language of his relatives and friends, as well as Richilo. In Britain he encounters a very different kind of culture, which is more media-based than oral, and almost anaemic in its language.

It is the narrator's relationship with the Rastafarian, Joseph, which foregrounds the importance of filmic images in the media-dominated culture of Britain. Joseph, being of African descent, is slightly peripheral to his Asian circle of friends. The reader is introduced to Joseph as someone who stands out: "The Home was unbearable. Of the fourteen boys, there were nine white, four black, and myself. Apart from Joseph, one of the blacks, the rest were impenetrable" (p.81). Though illiterate and always in trouble with the police, Joseph turns out to be the most imaginative of the boys. He has the most insight about language, and how words can be infinitely metaphorical:

> 'Words are so full of cleverness,' Joseph said, 'I wish I could learn how to read and write them. Every word is cat with nine separate lives, it come up to you for tickling and stroking and feeding, or it wander away and walk along neighbour's garden fence, or it crouch and concentrate when it see bird or it fall asleep under the bonnet of nearest parked car'. (p.103)

His observations form part of his contribution to a lively discussion with Shaz and the narrator on Conrad's *Heart of Darkness*. In the heat of the debate the narrator pays him this compliment, even if a silent, backhanded one: "And out of all this banal intro-spection he emerged with a glimmer of ideas which made me reach for my notepad" (p.100).

Joseph, however, succumbs to the lure of the media. One of the strands of the plot in the novel, in fact, concerns itself with his attempts, because of dissatisfaction with purely verbal analysis, to make a film about *Heart of Darkness* on the streets of London. The project becomes an obsession with him, but it leads him to a vision of nothingness, in which he glimpses horror similar to that of Kurtz in Conrad's work.

> Joseph pointed his camera for hours to an empty sky, lying on his back in Tooting Bec Common, careless of people walking their dogs, and the two tramps who at night slept in the public toilets adjoining the tennis courts and in the day-time journeyed from bin to bin. He had lost all curiosity in *things*. He no longer even wanted to steal a video player with which to view the images he was gathering on tape. He explained fitfully to Shaz and I why he had abandoned his Conrad project. By piecing his rambling explanations to-gether it became clear that he had developed an interest in nothingness, colourlessness, the sightlessness of air, wind, the pure space between trees rather than leaves clinging on to branches as if in terror of being blown away, or roots clutching frantically, digging down into the earth. (p.133)

Without realizing it, Joseph is doomed because of his belief that images captured through film are more reflective of reality than words. Just like the narrator, his intention is to 'make it' as an artist in society, but, as will be seen, his chosen medium be-trays him.

His reliance on film, and the narrator's on words, are tested when a chronically ill old woman, Ali the Asian landlord's sister, finally dies. The narrator, in a very traditional manner, decides to write an epitaph, but Joseph wants to film the funeral. It is at this point that the opposition between film as a documentary recorder of reality, and a *literary* genre is highlighted:

> Joseph diverted me by his own elaborate plans to film the funeral. It would be a more powerful statement on the old woman's life than any epitaph I could compose, he assured me. Once a silent admirer of books which I used to read aloud to him, he was now bold in his belief in the superiority of images, his increasing familiarity with the camera leading to a certain arrogance of outlook. (p.155)

The issue becomes a duel between the two, with the 'prize' being who can assuage Mr Ali's grief, and commemorate his sister better. Mr Ali, however, rejects Joseph's proposed film: "Not surprisingly Mr Ali would have none of Joseph's film, and was horrified when I asked him permission to bury it in his sister's coffin". (p.160)

The debate continues, but in the form of the narrator arguing for his different, indeed *textual* approach to commemorating the old woman's death:

> Mr Ali's sister would soon decompose to an unrecognizable mess, so what did the details of her appearance, her habits, her specific life, matter? The epitaph needed to be as universal as her bones. As soon as the idea came to me I knew I couldn't express it because the truth of his sister's fate, the very imagining of the way worms would arise in her flesh, the way it would loosen and leak, would distress him. Instead I evoked literary precedents, telling him of how Shakespeare did them, and Wordsworth. (p.161)

When Mr Ali pays the narrator for the epitaph, then he knows that he has found his writing vocation: "There was more to it than greed as I slipped the money into my pocket: I felt a real sense of achievement, of arrival, like a proper writer receiving his first down-payment". (p.162)

It becomes evident, in fact, that the narrator of *The Intended* forges his own individual identity out of literary texts. Joseph, on the other hand, fails because film turns out to be too treacherous a medium. He says at one point: "A film is like a mirror ... everybody who watch it see something different but is not necessarily what they want to see."(p.157) Joseph's observation is remarkably similar to what Walter Benjamin maintained about film-acting: "The feeling of strangeness that overcomes the actor before the camera ... is basically of the same kind as the estrangement felt before one's image in the mirror."[15] But unfortunately Joseph fails to see that film only mirrors the chaos and alienation within himself.

The narrator's other friend, Shaz, though in some ways as imaginative as Joseph, succumbs to hard-line, business-orientated materialism when he insists about words in the discussion on *Heart of Darkness* that "they are just a bunch of letters we form to identify things". (p.103) His imagination becomes more and more constricted, and by the end of the novel he appears to be interested in nothing more than making money and the crudest kind of sex. He combines the two interests by pimping for his girlfriend. He is, however, shown to be generous, to retain a sense of duty with regard to his family, and to have a shrewd sense of the dominance of money-orientated values in society. All these characteristics are evident in the following amusing excerpts:

> 'I'll lend you a fiver if you want,' he offered, and without waiting for my response, he fished out a wad of notes and peeled off two. 'Here, take ten, I've got loads.' I'd never seen so much cash in my life. He must have been holding a hundred pounds in his hands. 'It's Monica's money', he said, seeing the astonished expression on my face, 'she makes twice that in a week sometimes. I give thirty pounds a week

to my Mum to help her with the mortgage. She thinks I work
part-time at nights when I take Monica out. That's more than
what my Dad can give her on his wages. I give ten pounds to
my sister who's at college doing science.' It was as if he
wanted to reassure me that he was in moral control of his actions, that he still retained an Asian sense of duty to his
family. 'Everything in this country is about money,' he said,
suspecting that I still disapproved of his behaviour, 'you
don't want to be a Paki all your life. Here, take it,' and he
shoved the notes in my pocket. (pp.178-79)

He is, in short, possibly limited and certainly successful, and
Joseph unfortunately a dismal failure. The narrator values both of
them, and his 'intention', a very risky one, is to retain his imagination, but also to achieve financial and social success. He knows
perfectly well what the penalty for failure, even narrowly defined
in money terms, is in a harsh society, with Joseph's fate as a grim
warning. This is how he justifies his intention near the end of the
novel:

Patel's taunt that I want to become a white man is ridiculous. All I want is to escape from this dirt and shame called
Balham, this coon condition, this ignorance that prevents me
from knowing anything, not even who we are, who they are.
How else am I to make sense of what happened to Joseph?
The most important thing is to save myself from the misery
of his kind of being. (pp.230-31)

Having being ruptured from his society in Guyana, and being a
'dark stranger' in his adopted one,[16] he disciplines his imagination to provide him not only survival, but also success, through
the medium of literary texts.
   At one point, for instance, he identifies himself with Chaucer's
Criseyde because by allowing himself to be seduced by Shaz's
girlfriend, Monica, he has betrayed his own (Platonic) girlfriend,

Janet. When he does woo Janet, he tries Othello's technique (without actually mentioning him, but the allusion is transparent):

> My deepest wish was to move her to extreme emotion, to create laughter and sadness. It was obvious that I could not impress her with money, a privileged background, sartorial elegance, dancing skills or sheer handsomeness. All I had at my disposal was the gift of stories, the alien experiences of which would possibly seduce her, given her intelligent and enquiring nature. (p.125)

The novel, in fact, is studded with overt and direct literary references, but they are never superfluous, and always add to the reader's understanding of the characters, and their predicaments. The most illuminating of all the literary references consists of the extended discussion, which has already been mentioned, of *Heart of Darkness*, which reveals so much about Shaz, Joseph and the narrator himself.

Another important aspect of the literary references is that they make the narrator ultimately elusive, and much less of an idiosyncratic individual than the traditional hero of the 'bildungsroman'. He really has his being in the way he continually makes observations about great works of literature in order to arrive at self-definition. Even his friendships, particularly with Shaz and Joseph, he comes to consider as evanescent, almost superficial, because he has not really yet found himself:

> I've only known them on the surface, Shaz and Joseph. Now and again they would say and do something which would reveal some aspect of their character. But in the end all you've got left are a random collection of memories which you try to piece together into some grander truth. (p.216)

Like Walter Benjamin's film-actor, and as a result of the sheer struggle for survival *and* dignity, the narrator can only play himself, but it is a self still at an experimental stage. Significantly nameless, the narrator is very much in the position of a film-actor before a camera in a continual search for self-definition. In a sense, he really fears Joseph, because the Rastafarian, almost an alter-ego, reminds him of his own psychic divisions, exacerbated in a culture which apparently values media images above the realities of daily life.

Unlike Joseph, the narrator has his vivid memories, however "random", and however hard it may be to reintegrate them into "some grander truth", to sustain him. What happened to the child, and what happened to the adolescent have both contributed to the development of the budding writer looking back in Oxford, and Oxford is the *terminus,* where the narrator has "arrived" in more than one sense. But this does not mean that the narrator has entirely capitulated to 'white' values. He clearly still remains faithful to his past. This is why the novel ends with the narrator rejecting his idealization of his white girlfriend, Janet. He calls her, with Conradian irony, "the intended", and casts off his former unfocused self: "I didn't want to be born time and again. I didn't want to be an eternal, indefinite immigrant. I wanted to get off." (p.243) His former unfocused self, moreover, was not just the result of accidental circumstances, but also of neo-colonial stereotyping by the native English. Keeping this ending, and Joseph's suicidal fate, in mind, *The Intended* emerges just as subversive about British culture as Joyce's *Portrait of the Artist* was about Roman Catholicism in Ireland.

Notes

1   Something of what Dr Gilkes means by "creative schizophrenia" can be discerned in the following observation: "In the Caribbean the old schizophrenic dualism of 'two styles', of classical and creole, of standard and dialect, etc. is giving way to creative interpenetration. A contradictory culture is emerging which will no longer see itself as derived from a colonial history, but will impertinently reinterpret that history". See *Creative Schizophrenia: The Caribbean Cultural Challenge* (University of Warwick, 1986), p 15.

2   "Objective equivalent", and the much overused "objective correlative" are both phrases coined, at least in relation to literary criticism, by T S Eliot in his famous essay on *Hamlet*. Eliot's essay is of supreme importance in the analysis of West Indian writings because they are often in the position of Hamlet as Eliot interpreted him. He is a man so overwhelmed by angst that he cannot be objective about examining his own emotions. West Indian writers, including David Dabydeen, face a similar problem because they need to resolve psychic tensions arising from the brutalities of the slave era in Caribbean history. See 'Hamlet and His Problems' in T S Eliot, *The Sacred Wood* (London: Methuen & Co Ltd, 1920).

3   David Dabydeen, *Slave Song* (Mundelsrup, Denmark: Dangaroo Press, 1984), p 25.

4   *Slave Song*, p 13. See also David Dabydeen, 'On Not Being Milton: Nigger Talk in England Today' in *The State of the Language*, ed by Christopher Ricks and Leonard Michaels (London and Boston: Faber and Faber), p.1.

5   *Slave Song*, p.53.

6   See Benita Parry, 'Between Creole and Cambridge English: The Poetry of David Dabydeen' in this volume. Although my approach is somewhat different, I am highly indebted to Benita Parry's sensitive and pioneering work on David Dabydeen.

7   *Slave Song*, p.42.

8   David Dabydeen, *Coolie Odyssey* (London and Coventry: Hansib/ Dangaroo, 1988), p.9.

9   *Coolie Odyssey*, p.13.

10   *Coolie Odyssey*, p.7.

11   *Coolie Odyssey*, p.12.

12   See blurb at back of *Coolie Odyssey*.

13   *Coolie Odyssey*, pp.26-27.

14   David Dabydeen, *The Intended* (London: Secker & Warburg, 1991), pp. 27-28. All subsequent page references will be internal.

15   'The Work of Art in the Age of Mechanical Reproduction' in Walter Benjamin, *Illuminations*, trans. by Harry Zohn (London: Fontana/ Collins, 1973), p.232.

16   The title of an early sociological work on West Indian immigrants was as follows: *Dark Strangers: A Study of West Indians in London* (London: Pelican Books, 1963) by Sheila Patterson.

CHAPTER IX

NECROPHILIA OR STILLBIRTH? DAVID DABYDEEN'S
TURNER AS THE EMBODIMENT OF POSTCOLONIAL
CREATIVE DECOLONISATION

KAREN MCINTYRE

David Dabydeen's *Turner* is a complex and elusive work that
reflects and critically engages with some of the most pertinent issues surrounding postcoloniality and creativity as they are inscribed by the peculiar subject position of the relocated
Caribbean. The poem, framed by the lines "Stillborn from all the
signs" (I:1), and "No stars, no land, no words, no community,/No
mother" (XXV:855), records – as this essay seeks to show – the
imaginative and timeless struggle for creativity untainted by the
dis/ease of colonialism, a truly 'decolonised' postcolonial aesthetic in the face of a literally overwhelming wave of (neo)colonial
oppression, symbolised not only by the presence of the slaveship
itself, but also by the 'paedophilic' Turner.

Turner, by means of a series of strategic devices, aligns creativity with political imperatives, drawing inspiration from, and creatively challenging, particularities of colonial experience. These
devices include not only the attempt at an overcoming of pre-
scriptive modes of identification through an interrogation of what
it means to be at the margins of identity, but also the rewriting of
history via the creative re/membering of a series of 'plausible'
pasts, and the artful reworking of several pretexts. As Dabydeen
notes:

My poem focuses on the submerged head of the African in the foreground of Turner's painting. It has been drowned in Turner's (and other artists') seas for centuries. When it awakens it can only partially recall the sources of its life, so it invents a body, a biography, and peoples an imagined landscape.[1]

Taking the obscured submerged African head as its initial point of focus, the poem effectively navigates its way through a fictional and fictionalised odyssey of discovery, recuperation and transformation. This allows for a critical negotiation of the problematics of identity, history and creativity in its passage towards the full creative decolonisation that the work, on both a literal and literary level, serves to record.

(II)

As Slemon and Tiffin have illustrated, postcolonial writing is necessarily "grounded in the cultural realities of those societies whose subjectivity has been constituted at least in part by the subordinating power of European colonialism"[2], offering up the most practical site for the interrogation and countering of colonialism's most enduring characteristics. Postcolonial creative decolonisation must thus be a "process, not arrival" (*ibid*), for to arrive would be to reconfirm the (neo)colonialist system by replicating its ploy of facilitating an alternative static creative hegemony and thus providing a form of creative recolonisation from a different perspective. Strategically and politically dynamic, decolonisation is predicated upon the continual *overcoming* of these structures, combined with a critical interrogation of authority and priority, allowing for a distancing from the ideological and political imperatives of the metropolis.

One of the key features of creative decolonisation is its attempts to overcome the kinds of stereotypes characteristic of (neo)colonial discourse. Colonial discourse, as Bhabha asserts, is commonly seen to seek "authorisation for its strategies by the production of knowledge of colonizer and colonized which are stereotypical but antithetically evaluated"[3]. Dependent for its success on the perpetuation of clear distinctions between colo- niser and colonised, slave and master, it is through the unfixing of these binary configurations that effective decolonisation of impe- rialist-inspired cultural dominants would appear to lie. Yet these binaries would also seem to be a fundamental requirement for decolonising processes, for there has to be an 'other' to oppose and disarm. The decolonising intellectual requires a sense of op- position for her or his political or creative endeavour to succeed, the often relocated scholar or artist occupying a doubly ambiva- lent position of simultaneously attempting to dismantle untenable stereotypes based on segregation of racial, geographical or his- torically specific 'types', whilst trying to assert the de facto specificity and legitimacy of experience and tradition(s). As Radhakrishnan has suggested, the concept of identity is norma- tive in that it "totalizes heterogeneous 'selves' and 'subjectivi- ties', colonialism working to fix disparate identities to a particular location at a specific point in time, to homogenise heterogeneity."[4] There is no reason, however, why the copula 'is' cannot be re- placed with a more fluid 'both/and/neither/nor', a strategic anti- hegemonic device clearly apparent in *Turner*. Indeed, as Radhakrishnan has also noted:

> It is important to the postcolonial hybrid to compile a labori- ous "inventory of one's self" [or selves] and, on the basis of that complex genealogical process produce her own version of hybridity and find political legitimacy for that version. (*ibid*).

The notion of self, necessary for a sense of legitimacy and a po- sition from which to contest stereotypes, does not have to be based in simple essentiality but can be premised on a complex of

alternative selves. The vortex of competing "Turners" that informs
and motivates *Turner*, characterised by their insistent fluidity and
resistance to categorical containment, is suggestive of a creative
engagement with this 'legitimation crisis', allowing for decolonisation to be initiated without the negative repercussions of essen-
tialism which such manoeuvres tend to provoke. By the
deconstruction of stable notions of identity through the figure of
hybridity, (and at the same time the reassertion of binarism re-
vealed through this categorisation of hybrid 'types'), no fixed site
for being can be located. Ambivalence and the querying of the
limits of metropolitan conceptions of identity (through the poem's
oscillation between and intersplicing of differences and sameness) is one of the key pivots upon which the poem turns.

The use of "turns" here is intentional, the poem engaging not
only with what it means to be, but also playing with the boundaries around possibilities for meaning, and drawing attention towards the containment of the self and the power implicit within
language:

> ... Each night
> Aboard ship he gave selflessly the nipple
> Of his tongue until we learnt to say profitably
> In his own language, *we desire you, we love*
> *You, we forgive you* ...
> ... The more we struggled
> Ungratefully, the more steadfast his resolve
> To teach us words.
> (XXIV:795-804)

The enforcement of the language of the coloniser effects an ab-
sorption of its epithets of power. In opposition to this, one of *Turner's* strategies entails the uncovering of a multiplicity of
competing meanings for "Turner" submerged within both the text
and its context(s). "Turner" refers not only to the painter, but also

to many 'characters'[5] within the poem. Indeed the slaveship owner, an archetypal Imperialist and sometime paedophile, is Turner.

> ... He checks that we are parcelled
> In equal lots, men divided from women,
> Chained in fours and children subtracted
> From mothers. When all things tally
> He snaps the book shut, his creased mouth
> Unfolding in a smile, as when, entering
> His cabin, mind heavy with care, breeding
> And multiplying percentages, he beholds
> A boy dishevelled on his bed...
> (XII:324-332)

Turner's children are also "Turner", a progeny comprised not only of J.M.W. Turner's paintings which he liked to refer to as his "children"[6], but also of a particular "part-born" child, the product of a liaison with a black female slave aboard the craft.

Thus "Turner" simultaneously occupies several positions of authority whilst at the same time being located in a space lacking authority, a place without presence. The child is part-born and exists only as an ambivalent essence upon which a will-to-life has been imposed, not inherently given. The child Turner is ripe for "naming" and instruction, able to be known only as a point of reference for others, putting those others in – to borrow from Said – a whole series of possible relationships without ever losing them the upper hand. Here the dominant identity gains strength and fixity by setting itself off against this alien other as a surrogate, underground self that is the same yet different, almost but not quite. By being located paradoxically both at the point of absence and presence, *Turner* simultaneously avows and disallows the authorities that lie within and between each separate or interconnected persona the game of naming permits.

Refiguring and reconceptualising both Turner senior and his "children" in an act that is both necrophilial or appropriative – borrowing from canonical pretexts – and uniquely creative, *Turner* enacts a complex and intricate decolonising of both the strategies of (neo)colonialism and their postcolonial restaging; performing what Wilson Harris has described as an "Infinite Rehearsal"[7], a continuous repetition, with difference, of the major strategies of a particular discursive practice in order to disempower and subvert them, the emphasis being on a self-exploratory as well as oppositional critical investigation.

The self-conscious ambivalencing that the characterisation within the poem supports is further complicated by the ambiguity of the child, who is both neither/nor and both/and. The product of black, white, coloniser, colonised, (and, furthermore, a metonym for the poem itself and the process of postcolonial creativity *per se)* it is stillborn. By inserting a series of alternative "Turners" into the work, the whole spectrum of colonial, neocolonial and postcolonial activity – from oppression to resistance and overcoming – is palimpsestically and intricately refigured. In this way, the poem propagates and promotes the unfixing of the notion of the stability of identities, the discourses that inform them, and throws into doubt the 'legitimacy' of authoritative readings of itself. This playing permits, on a theoretical and creative level, the aligning of black slave and notions of active colonialism, and vice versa, ultimately disallows containment and the limits or boundaries that enforce it. By disallowing simplistic oppositions through this playful and anarchic negotiation between pretext, text and context, the poem reveals how the agency of the relocated postcolonial is both split between, and doubled at the dual sites of creative articulation. The process of decolonisation is thus in itself fluid, situated not solely at the site of 'author' or at the site of 'meaning'.

(III)

The decolonising manoeuvres of *Turner* are not restricted to the interrogation and revisualising of identity, but also work through the recrafting or reviewing of canonical pretexts, not least 'Slavers'. Curiously, this painting, (striking not only because of its overtly controversial subject matter but also in terms of the way in which it is painted[8]), has, whilst being praised or condemned in aesthetic terms, been virtually ignored regarding its central theme of slavery and the Middle Passage. Both Gilroy[9] and Dabydeen draw attention to this anomaly, Dabydeen noting that although Ruskin "Wrote a detailed account of the composition of the painting, [...] Its subject, the shackling and drowning of Africans, was relegated to a brief footnote" adding that "the footnote reads like an afterthought, something tossed overboard"[10].

Whilst this fragment of information may seem in itself of marginal significance, both margins and footnotes are in fact of considerable importance both to this study and its primary material. As Wilson Harris has noted, footnotes, whilst appearing of only secondary interest, are often of more importance than the main body of text. One needs, he writes, to examine them "closely in the context of events to begin to perceive their enormous significance"[11]. Indeed, it is non-metropolitan versions of history, culture and creative tradition that have, until recently, been marginalised out of Western accounts of the past. Therefore, rather than seeing footnotes as supplementary and 'after the fact' of the main text, they should perhaps be viewed as in fact *prior* to it, signalling and attending to the always-already-there absences or gaps the main work supports and perpetuates. Seen this way, footnotes become the lost history and culture, the 'holes' in standard representations, that once retrieved and reinserted, allow one to write and read otherwise, against the dominant order, in an essentially decolonising fashion. As Ngugi wa Thiong'o has noted, "moving the centre to correct the imbalance of the last four hundred years is a crucial step" in the direction of cultural freedom[12].

Such a motion or crosscurrent, with its interrupting of the dominant flow of both scholarship and hegemonic cultural practice, held in conjunction with the notion of reading or writing otherwise, provides a useful modelling[13] of one of the creative strategies of *Turner*, which clearly contributes to this process towards cultural freedom through its revisioning of 'Slavers'. Focusing on the submerged African head in the foreground yet periphery of the painting, *Turner* enacts a deliberate movement of the centre from the white, colonial west, to the black, colonised so-called margin: a 'plugging' (in both senses of the word) of a prevailing 'hole' in Western versions of colonial history with a clear postcolonial political imperative.

Significantly, this choice of focus finds its very locus in an absent presence, for the head in fact remains unseen in Turner's work. All that is visible above sea level in the painting is, fittingly, a foot, and by placing this 'footnote' in primary position as protagonist, not only is an active re-ordering of the dominant power structure effected, but also its undoing. In an original and productive refiguring of what is in danger of itself becoming a 'canonised' decolonising strategy[14], Dabydeen provides an appropriation and abrogation of hegemonic creative formations through an imaginative engagement and recrafting both of this culturally significant painting and the decolonisation of the assumed subject positions that inform it. Instead of the critical and imaginatively necrophilial engagement with the artefacts of the past resulting in a stale and unproductive creativity – a form of stillbirth – the emphasis is firmly shifted to a counter-perception, despite a history of Western 'forgetting', of aporia; creativity is *still*born.

This struggle between oppositions and their undoing reflects, and is reflected in, Turner's painting, where drowning slaves, various "Turners", and the colonisers' and coloniseds' histories are intermingled in a visual and intellectual synergy that prohibits a separating out of competing antithetical identities or constructs. As Jack Lindsay has noted:

An iridescent hole of light is the point to which all forms are
related [...] It is not a simple passage in-and-through; it continually involves a tension of contrary pulls or motions, of
which the head-on collision of wind and tide is the plainest
example, but which is to be found in all sorts of meetings,
mergings, thwartings, involvements, resistances, clashes between two forces or movements[15].

Lindsay's comments are extremely pertinent. His description
of the hole of light is particularly suggestive of the 'holes' or footnotes in historical accounts of colonial activity and their plugging, the unifactory light synthesising 'different' colonial and
postcolonial accounts of history through an *otherwise* reading,
reinserting the absent other in a 'moving of the centre'. With the
coloniser's slaveship situated on one side and the colonised
slaves on the other in an oppositional formation – the coloniser
placed in a higher position than the drowning slaves – resolution
comes not through the defeat of one by the other, but through the
necrophilial synthesis of the two into a creative whole, the figure
of the sun drawing both together. This creative refashioning is
clearly thematised in the poem, the slave debating whether to embark on a creative liaison with an 'Other' 'text'.

Shall I call to it even as the dead
Survive catastrophe to speak in one
Redemptive and prophetic voice, even
As a jackal breathing into bone
Rouses familiar song?
(XX:579-583)

The "jackal breathing into bone", suggests the 'bone flute'[16], a
creative tool fashioned out of the carcass of the opponent, indicat-
ing a form of creativity that is *still*born rather than stillborn. By
eating the flesh of the enemy and by refashioning one of his or her

bones into a flute, new cross-cultural creativity can arise out of conflict, oppositions refigured into a creative syncretism signalling the emergence of new cultural formations. The bone flute figures as the necrophilial key to mutual spaces, providing a threshold into creativity. Dabydeen fashions *Turner* from the "bones" of the past, creating a new work of art, a new cultural product. Consuming and appropriating "the dead" – both artist and the subject of his art: colonialism – in an act of creative necrophilia, Dabydeen "suckles" his work on "tales of resurrected folk" (XX:583-4); taking his inspiration not just from the real dead, but also the dead he has himself created, enacting a double creation/consumption. Manu is 'killed off' by the poet, providing an opportunity for the dead slave to "Invent a sister, and another, as Manu would" (XX:585). The act of simultaneous creation and aborted creation – the paradox of being (*still*) stillborn – is rehearsed, repeated and finds its fruition in the various figures of "Turner" and *Turner*.

Creativity and the need to create in the face of an increasing sense of impotence is highly thematised in *Turner*; creativity is painful, frequently violent and explosive, fraught with the danger of failure – of being stillborn – and invariably linked to historical experience:

> ... First a woman sobs
> Above the creak of timbers and the cleaving
> Of the sea, sobs from the depths of true
> Hurt and grief, as you will never hear
> But from woman giving birth, belly
> Blown and flapping loose and torn like sails,
> Rough sailors' hands jerking and tugging
> At ropes of veins to no avail. Blood vessels
> Burst asunder, all below deck are drowned.
> (I: 1-9)

In this case, creativity and its success are controlled by, and at the mercy of, the coloniser, premised on seduction or rape, and resulting in both enslavement and apparent indebtedness to the colonial master: the creation thrown overboard. Articulation outside of or beyond the cultural hegemony does not signify:

> Turner crammed our boys' mouths too with riches,
> His tongue spurting strange potions upon ours
> Which left us dazed, which made us forget
> The very sound of our speech.
> (XXIV:792-795)

There are, as the conclusion of the poem informs the reader, "No words, no community,/No mother" (XXV:881-5).

Through the absence of language comes absence itself, the part-born present only by its very absences, reconstituting itself through the appropriation of an/other's label: "Nigger". Yet this does not necessarily signify stillbirth. The absence of history, tradition and origin, whilst suggesting a lack, also reveals free-floating signification, a liberation from constraint. Focusing on the tension between freedom and constraint, creativity and impotence, the part-born, as both the product of cross-cultural imagination and impetus for postcolonial creativity, provides a complex motif for creativity and its productions:

> ... it dips
> Below the surface, frantically it tries to die,
> To leave me beadless, nothing and a slave
> To nothingness, to the white enfolding
> Wings of Turner brooding over my body,
> Stopping my mouth...
> (XXV:828-833)

Articulating the desire for an independent creativity and its struggle against defeat whilst also, through its echo of Yeats'

'Leda and the Swan', suggesting a complicit creativity, these lines rehearse the problems and possibilities inherent within a hybrid creative form. *Turner*, through its engagement with Yeats, can be understood as perhaps claiming solidarity with other colonised peoples. The duplicitous final stanza of 'Leda and the Swan' – the poem itself a rewriting – can be seen to suggest not only the negative aspects of domination/colonisation as figured in the rape, but the possibility for positive creativity to emerge from violence:

> Being so caught up,
> So mastered by the brute blood of the air,
> Did she put on his knowledge with his power
> Before the indifferent beak could let her drop?

'Knowledge' can be used advantageously; Leda founded Greek civilisation. Knowledge of (neo)colonialism, English, of canons and canonical forms can be used for decolonising purposes, to subvert that very knowledge implicit in Yeats' poem. Yet this rehearsal, as imitation, can also lead to neocolonialism. Once again creativity is seen as a violent act, premised on a violation or violent seduction. The divisions between coloniser and colonised, collusive and oppositional creativity, necrophilia and *still*birth, are once again blurred, the part-born, a potential slave, leaving his adoptive "mother" "nothing and a slave/To nothingness" (XXV:830-831). Marked both by "riches" and "barrenness" (XXI:701) the ambivalencing is clarified: they are "One and the same pathway" (*ibid*: 702).

(IV)

Rediscovered in *Turner* is the past, both real and fictional, crafted through an acknowledgement but superseding of Western culture. "History", both as the West's account of, and the colonised's experience of the past, is subjected to interrogation and transformation through the multiple and fragmented 'characters' "Turner" supports and the manifold displacements that this fluidity echoes. Realist narrative is replaced by series of 'plausible stories' implemented through the narrator's multiplicitous invention of a "body, a biography"[17] that disturb notions of linearity and progress, the defining tropes of colonialist and neocolonial thought. This naming, involving a process of labelling that echoes colonial strategies of containment, of appropriation of the other for the self, is here refigured as a reclaiming, a reappropriation of a lost past, culture and traditions through imagination, postcolonial creativity signalled and initiated by the naming of the part-born at a time when the namer has "forgotten the words" (XII:344). *Still* born despite the experience of colonial enslavement, yet still born only part-born, a "morsel slipped from the belly of moon" (XVI:496), the slave-protagonist names it:

> ... Turner
> As I have given fresh names to birds and fish
> And humankind, all things living but unknown,
> Dimly recalled, or dead.
> (I:22-25)

Turner, through the African slave's reminiscences, repeatedly rehearses the part-born's "birth" into the sea of memory, yet these repetitions do not just refocus attention on the past, but permit cathartic, creative overcoming:

> ... the child
> Floats towards me, bloodied at first, but the sea
> Will cleanse it.
> (IX:248-250)

The negative aspects of colonial activity are not, however, 'washed over' in a suppression of history. The poem, rather engages with, and focuses on the contention between creative re/membering and forgetting:

> ... I wanted to teach it
> A redemptive song, fashion new descriptions
> Of things, new colours fountaining out of form.
> I wanted to begin anew in the sea
> But the child would not bear the future
> Nor its inventions, and my face was rooted
> In the ground of memory...
> (XXV: 815-821).

The postcolonial process of giving things their names is self-consciously explored within *Turner* by the part-born rejecting labelling by others for self-naming, baptising himself and his new "mother" with a name tainted by, yet nourished by cultural and historical reality:

> ... 'Nigger!' it cried, seeing
> Through the seas' disguise as only children can,
> Recognising me below my skin long since
> Washed clean of the colour of sin, scab, smudge...
> (XI:281-284)

> ... 'Nigger'
> It cries, naming itself ...
> (XXV:826-827)

The attempt at a forgetting or re/solving and dis/solving of the past through renaming is stillborn, thwarted by recognition of the self and experience (XVIII:496). As Dabydeen notes:

> [The slave's] real desire is to begin anew in the sea but he is too trapped by grievous memory to escape history. Although the sea has transformed him – bleached him of colour and complicated his sense of gender – he still recognises himself

as 'nigger'. The desire for transfiguration or newness or creative amnesia is frustrated.

There is no pure expression untainted, or uninfluenced by colonial activity. Modern postcolonial or neocolonial creativity is contingent to some extent on necrophilial associations.

Moving another 'footnote' to the body of the text, both the slave protagonist and Dabydeen enact a retrieval from the 'white washing' ocean of history "which Turner vandalised/With a great sweep of his sword in search/Of his own fables" (XIX:569-574). Just as the African slave's creation of two sisters can be read as symbolic of the process of postcolonial creativity through retrieval and imitation/abrogation, so too *Turner*, through its creation of plausible stories about people and their possible past(s) can be seen to reflect this process, operating by way of the retrieval of a barren history through imaginative re/membering, providing a fictionalised version of a given reality. As the narrator says of future generations:

> ... Each
> Will be barren of ancestral memory
> But each endowed richly with such emptiness
> From which to dream, surmise, invent, immortalise.
> Though each will wear different coloured beads
> Each will be Manu, the source and future
> Chronicles of our tribe.
> (XXI:726-731)

Dabydeen reinscribes both the postcolonial rewriter and colonial writer of history into the work through the figure of the solitary vulture, reconfirming the similarity within difference, the dual applications of an identical tactical device:

> A solitary vulture dips into one's fresh breast
> As into an ink-well, wipes its beak upon

Another's parchment skin, writing its own
Version of events...
(XVIII:520-523)

Writing through the memory of a victim who is yet heroic, the
memories triggered by the surrender of this part-born to the sea,
memories both fictional and fictionalised, reveal both a forgotten
and deliberately suppressed past life where "nothing has re-
mained/original" and speech "mocks the present and time/To
come" (X:257-258; 263-264).

(V)

Creative decolonisation involves:

> The dis/mantling, de/mystification and unmasking of Euro-
> pean authority [...] and the retrieval or creation of an inde-
> pendent identity.[18]

Turner moves away from realist representation; resists closure;
exposes the politics of metaphor and permits an abrogation of binary structuring through a series of imaginatively employed strategies. These manoeuvres, including not only the provision of a
multiplicity of competing alternative "Turners", but also an inter-
rogative recrafting of canonical pretexts and concomitant plugging
of the 'holes' in standard representations of the past through the
creative revisioning of History, serve both to reveal and provide a
completely envisaged and sophisticated journey into creative decolonisation.

Negotiating en route the consequent complications of necrophilia and stillbirth, *Turner* reminds us all, how, despite History
and the hegemonic West, and perhaps in contradiction to the
words of its own ambivalent narrator, Caribbean writing has nevertheless, "remained/original" (X:257-8).

Notes

1   *Turner* (London: Jonathan Cape, 1994), p. ix.

2   S. Slemon and H. Tiffin, *After Europe* (Sydney: Dangaroo Press, 1989). p. ix.

3   H. Bhabha, *The Location of Culture* (London: Routledge, 1994), p.70.

4   R. Radhakrishnan, 'Postcoloniality and the Boundaries of Identity', in *Callaloo*, Vol.16, No.4, 1993, pp. 750-771.

5   'Character' is used advisedly, for want of a more conceptually appropriate term.

6   See Jack Lindsay's work on Turner: *Turner*, (London: Panther, 1966).

7   Wilson Harris, *The Infinite Rehearsal* (London: Faber & Faber, 1987).

8   Jack Lindsay notes how Turner's colour structure in 'Slavers' and other similar pieces "break[s] through all the prevailing concepts and limitations of method", *ibid*, p. 223.

9   Paul Gilroy, *Small Acts* (London: Serpent's Tail, 1993), p.81.

10   *Turner*, p. ix.

11   Wilson Harris, *Explorations* (Sydney: Dangaroo Press, 1981), p.10.

12   Ngugi wa Thiong'o, *Moving the Centre* (London: Currey, 1993), p. xvii.

13   'Modelling' is a particularly precarious term due to its connotations of containment and control, and the effective neocolonisation of the text it can be seen to imply. Clearly this is not the intention here, the emphasis is on this being one of a variety of possible ways into the poem, which quite evidently through its own set of strategies, works to resist ultimate restriction to a particular, authoritative meaning.

14   Postcolonial canonical rewriting has become the main focus of the majority of analyses of counter-discursive strategies, and whilst this is obviously a valid and important area of postcolonial creativity – with writers as diverse as Rhys, Coetzee and Walcott having utilised such a technique – the assertion of this as the primary tool for anti-hegemonic writing is problematic. Not only does such a 'canonisation' disempower the manoeuvre – it is after all, meant as a subversive strategy not a mainstream device, also implying a tacit collusion between the postcolonial and the very thing s/he is writing against – it also relegates other equally important creative strategies to a more marginal position, thereby categorising them as being of less importance or significance.

15   Jack Lindsay, *op.cit.*, pp. 213-4.

16   See Wilson Harris: *The Womb of Space: The Cross Cultural Imagination* Westport: (Connecticut: Greenwood, 1983).

17   *Turner*, p.ix.

18   Helen Tiffin, 'Post-Colonialism, Post-Modernism and the Rehabilitation
      of Post-Colonial History', in *Journal of Commonwealth Literature*, Vol.
      23, No.7, pp. 169-181.

CHAPTER X

INTERVIEW WITH DAVID DABYDEEN,
1989

WOLFGANG BINDER

WB *In which sense is Guyana unique as far as the Caribbean is concerned?*

DD Undoubtedly in that it possesses a landscape and an interior that are different from the rest of the English-speaking islands. You have an interior that is jungle. Its very presence provokes myths that have to do with pre-Columbian culture. We still have an Amerindian population. You get a sense that Guyana is more ancient than the rest of the anglophone Caribbean; also, because we do not have a tourist trade, it is easier for indigenous things to survive. The influences from outside are not as overt or traumatic as, say, in Barbados. So Indians could remain Indians for a longer period, Hinduism and Islam could continue to flourish, or people could control the pace of change as they become more and more creolized. They are in control of the process to a greater degree anyway than in Jamaica or Barbados.

WB *What were some of your first impressions of England?*

DD I think there was the fascination with brick buildings. I had never seen brick before. In Guyana it is wood, or mud, or concrete. I had never seen brick buildings joined together – this was fascinating. Then, I suppose, one of the things that was precious to us: apples, red apples, which we used to get for Christmas. They were abundant in England, so you were impressed by the abundance of these fruits which were precious· in Guyana. And something which affects, I suppose, all West Indians, the sight of snow, the absolute magic of that. The images of apples and snow are important because it was very much part of the imagery which had to do with the England we grew up imagining. England was a place that had to do with snow, apples, and of course daffodils. I remember reading, when I was a boy, about English children in our story books. And they would have tea at about five, and they would have scones. And I always wondered what scones were until I came to England. Those images, when they become real, were very disappointing, even the magical snow. After a while the apples became boring, and the scones turned out to be tasteless buns and the snow was cold. But that is part of the naïveté of it. In terms of a continuity in my youth there was always a sense of violence, the sense of violence that I had as a child in the racial turmoil in Guyana of the sixties. When you came to Britain, you had the same sense of displacement, and there was always the threat of violence. I grew up at a time when the skinheads were very strong and influential. I grew up when Enoch Powell made those very provocative speeches, like "We need to expel immigrants from the host body". So we as immigrant children were subdued by the threat of violence, which was a terrible thing to have to grow up with. It really must influence the way you look at the world, and also what you write.

WB *As you see it today, were your parents naïve in coming to England? Would they see England as an opulent mother country waiting for them, or were they realistic in that they knew that they would have to fight for every bit of advancement?*

DD   I think that my parents, and other people's parents, would
     have seen England not quite as an Utopia, or an El Dorado
     in reverse, but certainly as a place where jobs were plentiful
     and the people hospitable, and wealth within your grasp. I
     think there was the belief that if you went to England and
     worked, you could become wealthy, whereas in fact, when
     they came, they were not welcome as they expected to be.
     Sam Selvon documented this very well in his novels. I think
     what they did not reckon on was the sense of humiliation in
     being an immigrant and a colonial. That would have never
     entered their minds or their vision, that they would wear a
     badge of shame. And also that they would be constantly re-
     minded by the host society that they were in some ways un-
     wanted and they would have to carry that burden of guilt and
     shame with them.

WB   *Would they talk about that, in the house?*
DD   No, we talked about it as children. Because I went about
     with Asian boys of my age – I went to a boys' school – and
     the Asian boys were very ashamed, as I was, when we
     walked home from school and saw a couple of Asian women
     in saris who obviously looked different. We always felt
     ashamed and we would talk about that to each other: "I wish
     they wouldn't wear saris", even though we were talking
     about our own mothers; "I wish they would put dresses on".
     Or we would be ashamed if we were in a train carriage or in
     a bus, and two Asians spoke loudly or audibly in Urdu or
     whatever. As little boys, we wished they would keep quiet. In
     other words, there was very great pressure among us to
     become invisible. We never talked to the parents about this.
     I think for that reason we became integrated, in a negative
     sense, as rapidly as possible, when we grew up. We would
     put little earrings in our ears, or smoke a bit of dope, or we
     would go dancing or argue the merits of David Bowie's
     music against that of T Rex. It was out of that pressure to

integrate. And what is sad is that it meant that as soon as you had the freedom to leave your parents, you dropped as quickly as possible that which was Asian about yourself. You stopped eating curry, if necessary! You did not want to be different or to be defined as "other". I must say that subsequently, twenty years later, in the eighties, I can now be proud and call myself Asian, an Asian-Caribbean person, or have close friends who are Asians who have their saris and their turbans. You can do that now, because the community is much stronger. In many instances we actually run this society. We have rejuvenated whole areas of British industry, we are well-represented at the universities, we have a lot more money in our pockets. With that stability we can actually be proud of promoting ancestral values. Now I cannot speak for all of them, but you will not find the new generation of Asians with that same sense of guilt and shame. If anything, things go the opposite way; it is a sense of superiority over English indecencies or the lack of excellence in English culture. The Asian writers think that they are better than the English writers in the English language. And the scientists think that they are better at Western science than the Whites. So we have gone from a sense of humiliation to a sense of, maybe, false pride and self-assertion.

WB *Your own career can be called at least a double one. Were there people who were instrumental in putting you into prestigious universities?*

DD No, quite the opposite. I grew up in South London, a stone's throw away from Brixton. I grew up in the care of the local authorities, because my parents were divorced. I was living in an environment without parental protection or financial resources, because I was totally dependent upon the state for a weekly cheque. Between the ages of fourteen and eighteen, if you don't have a measure of self-discipline, you are finished. It was really as bleak as that. What motivated me really was a sense that I did not want to be poor; I did not want to be an immigrant, and there was no way that I was going to leave school and work in a shop, or work on a bus or a train. Nor did I want to go to any university but Oxford or Cambridge. It was not sufficient for me to go to the University of Warwick or the University of Surrey. It had to be Oxford or Cambridge, because if I was to survive and to progress from the conditions in which I was living at the time, I might as well aim for the very 'best'. I had nothing to lose. I did not have any special tuition in school apart from the interest and memorable generosity of a white English teacher who pushed me towards English literature and gave me extra lessons. He was an erudite and inspiring teacher – Mr Mulhern was his name. If Cambridge had rejected me, I would have been without a university place. It really was a decision to be extreme. I had absolute good fortune, and it worked! I was interviewed by dons, who obviously exercised a degree of compassion and balanced academic capacities against social background. I think I got in by an absolute stroke of luck. Of course, I did also pass the necessary exams.

WB *You published two books on English art, on Hogarth. What made you interested in British art?*

DD We grew up in the Caribbean without a visual memory. In Guyana I could never remember seeing any African image apart from the bodies of the people. There was nothing like African painting in the house, there was nothing like Indian art in the house. The closest you could get to Indian images were the pictures of deities. One's visual field was dominated by Christian, Western images, either by the copies of Constables or the pictures of Jesus. I decided to have a closer look at these images that in a superficial way had dominated my childhood. It led to a deeper inquiry into the nature of British art.

WB *Could you share a few insights on your work on Hogarth?*

DD I can't really look at British art without finding something of
myself in it, or, if not myself, of the people that I come from.
The first book was called *Hogarth's Blacks.* It was an attempt
to highlight those marginal black figures in Hogarth's canvases, to take them out of the canvases, to examine why they
were there, how they were meshed in with the total narrative,
what Hogarth was saying about the black presence. It was an
attempt to show that English art has a dimension of blackness to it; in other words, and on a personal level, that I belonged to British society. Now, art is very precious, and art
history is a very genteel occupation, and the emblems of
English civilization are its paintings, its art galleries, and
you have to insert your blackness there. It's almost like
gaining entrance to Cambridge. You had to take what was defined as English high culture and try to find yourself in
there. Looking at Hogarth, I saw there were all these black
marginalized figures populating his paintings. But looking
closely at them, one saw how they were very much part of
the complexity of the narrative, they had stories, Hogarth
had endowed them with narratives. It was a matter of finding
out about Hogarth and his purposes and trying to fit the
Black into his narrative design. The second book, *Hogarth,
Walpole and Commercial Britain*, was really about Hogarth's
treatment of the working classes. And again I could find myself in that in terms of sympathy with the kinds of people he
painted: the prostitutes, the beggars, on the whole the dis-
possessed. In other words, the academic work that I have
been doing on eighteenth-century England has never been
divorced from a personal quest to belong to twentieth-cen-
tury England.

WB *When you say that you want to "belong", that you wish to be
a part of British society, isn't there a loyalty conflict or a tension between the British Isles and Guyana?*

DD   Well, I tend to think that Britain depended upon us heavily for its material and cultural advance. So when I say that I want to belong, I mean I want to recognize that. To recognize that I (and by "I" I don't mean just myself, but the tribe) have had a very important say and impact in their development. The sense of belonging only comes about when the British recognize that. So there is not a tension in that way. Ultimately, you come to a kind of vision: our cultures have become so intimately enmeshed over the centuries, that you cannot be Guyanese without being British, and you cannot be British without being Guyanese or Caribbean.

WB   *Would you see yourself in a certain opposition with writers like Kamau Brathwaite, who finds and recreates Africa in the Caribbean, in part via a mythical procedure?*

DD   I don't think that the connection I seek with British culture negates the connection with, in my case, Indo-Caribbean culture. I am not saying that the two pursuits are mutually exclusive. I think it is absolutely essential to embark upon the kind of project that Brathwaite has embarked upon, which is the recognition and rediscovery of the Africanness of the region. Brathwaite has said that the Africanness does not necessarily reside in books or in paintings. It might reside in a headdress worn by a Caribbean woman; it might reside in a few words that are said that have survived the Middle Passage; a cobweb reminds him of the Anansi myth. These are absolutely crucial recollections, because the alternative is a surrender to metropolitan values. I think you can discover that your ancestral identity has modified the metropolitan identity. I would not hold, however, to the view – as I think C L R James has expressed it – that we are creatures that have been created by the West. I think that is a profoundly limited view of the Caribbean psyche, of Caribbean sensibility, or of Caribbean culture. I am an Indian in many ways; I can be obsessed at times by notions of purity. Now this isn't Brahminical, because I don't think I come from a Brahminical caste, but sometimes I think these notions of purity go back to Indian rituals of purification. My sense of family, I am sure, is a very Indian attribute. Those are just two examples. So what has Europe to do with that?

WB *Do you have any idea why Guyana has become such a fertile country on the literary landscape? Guyana has since the fifties produced an astonishing number of good writers.*

DD I think there are two reasons: one, that politically, we had a more traumatic history than many islands. We had the first elected Marxist government in that part of the world, if not in any part of the world. This was in the 1950s, when Cheddi Jagan and the People's Progressive Party won election after election, which created all kinds of tensions with Britain, so that in 1953 the British suspended our constitution, and sent the troops in, and occupied us, and locked up the poets, like Martin Carter, who then created memorable poetry out of that experience of imprisonment. Art emerges more readily out of volatility. But then, secondly, I think that having a continental landscape, having an interior, has provoked and fed the literary imagination. You have to imagine that we are wedged between jungle and the Atlantic Ocean. We live in a thin strip of coast in Guyana. And that sense of being an island on land must provoke the imagination, it must trigger off all kinds of mythic quests and visions. I think that these are some of the factors that have created the peculiar literature of Guyana, but the literature from Guyana is no more varied in subject matter – it is different – no greater in quantity or varied in subject matter than the literature in Trinidad, say. What we have to ask is: how come in the last thirty or forty years we have seen such an enormous growth of literature from the West Indies? I don't think there is any other region on earth that has in a short period of time pro-

duced such world-class writers. These are writers who are
now considered the very best writers in the English language.

WB *I am sure you know the chapter that V S Naipaul inserted in
his book, 'The Middle Passage'. Were you stung by his remarks?*

DD What was useful about those commentaries, I think, was his
perception that race would eventually destroy the society.
His novel *The Mimic Men* is inspired by Guyanese experiences. Whatever Naipaul is, he is an acute, analytical observer, and he was able to prophesy that the racial division
would lead to a kind of backwardness, economic and moral,
which it has led to. But there were also gentle parts in the
essay. I think Naipaul was probably more gentle in that book
than in most of his others. I remember his beautiful portrait
of Cheddi Jagan and Janet Jagan, and the feeling that the
whole country was being run by a husband and his wife, run
almost like a family, where the nationalization of some major
business concern seemed like a homely domestic transaction.

WB *I would like to move on to your career as a writer. My question is not a particularly original one, but I'm going to ask it
anyway. When did you start writing, and did you always
write in the poetic mode?*

DD I suppose it is a clichéd answer, but I always wrote since I
can remember. I remember Naipaul saying that if he couldn't
write, he would die, and when I heard that – I was young
then – I agreed with him. And I don't think it has anything
to do with ego. Guyana is a highly literate society, consider-
ing the lack of resources and various deprivations. Reading
was as natural as eating. In terms of the form, I think most
West Indian writers have begun as poets: Wilson Harris was
a poet, Sam Selvon wrote poetry, and George Lamming, even
Naipaul wrote a bit of poetry before coming to Europe where

fiction was the dominant mode, where fiction had the status, and was considered spacious enough to tell the whole story of the Caribbean. I myself have moved into fiction now. I have not written a poem for about a year, in part just to give fiction a go. It is largely also a surrender to the pressures to write fiction, and there is the sense, too, of the challenge of a new art form.

WB *Could you mention the overall concept of your first book, 'Slave Song'?*

DD Well, it is really in the title, slave and song, the contradiction between the two. What I wanted to show was the way of life that survived brilliantly and wickedly, mischievously and tragically, in spite of certain experiences of violence and brutality. Somehow human life and the sense of the comic in life survives everything. Although many of the poems dealt with starkly pornographic experiences, what Wilson Harris calls "the pornography of empire", I hope that I dealt with them with a kind of detached comedy or a kind of wit that converted the seriousness of pornographic intent into the mischief of the human spirit. So you have people celebrating their sexual powers in spite of being tied down, or whipped, or beaten. They refuse to be impotent. They celebrate their penises, they celebrate their lust for the white woman, the mistress of the plantation, which is their way of getting even with the plantation owner. They can't sleep with her, but they can lust for her, and there is no way that the plantation owner can erase that lust from their minds. Of course politically correct theorists will denounce such lust as pernicious; but what do they know about that kind of living? Or about anything real for that matter?

WB *This first book of poetry of yours is a volume that has an introduction, notes; it even has translations.*

DD A lot of that was playful. People like Brathwaite have been arguing for years that Creole is a different language, sufficiently different from English to be considered its own language. So therefore the logic would be to provide a translation, which is what I did. But many of the notes are spoof notes: they are almost saying that I want to be the critic as well as the poet. This is not because I like criticism, but it is just that I felt I would do the whole lot, and the poems would almost be minimalist poems. What mattered were not just the poems, but the notes to the poems. None of the poems uses the word "I"; one inhabits a series of masks, and the notes were my way of saying, "Look, I am just rendering history; look, I am the critic". Of course, this is a complete illusion, a farce.

WB *Would you say there is in using this procedure a danger of reducing the poems as texts?*

DD Yes, but it is important that you should raise the whole question of a poem as a poem and a poem as a text. And you raise questions about the reception of Caribbean poetry. I am concerned about the critical business that thrives upon the expression of poverty or of dispossession, which is what the Caribbean voice ultimately is. And, in my next book, *Coolie Odyssey*, I end the long title poem not by asking who I am writing for, but by saying. "Look, I am writing and they are consuming it". And what are they consuming? They are consuming poverty, the poverty of the tribe. So all these ironies are fascinating, and the purpose of the notes was also to raise these issues of critical consumption.

WB *I read the notes almost on the same level as the poetry, which makes for a very interesting interplay. Poem and comment become an intertextual affair.*

DD Yes, and people have said to me: "Oh, you should not have added the notes", but I found writing the notes as complex and as fascinating as writing the poems.

WB   *I would like to hear you on the use of Creole, its effects and the psychology behind it.*

DD   If you are to write about the lives of, say, the cane cutters, the use of their language, it seems to me, can be essential. Wordsworth said that poetry was the language of ordinary men. His own poetry wasn't, and my Creole isn't, because you always shape the language you use. I am not so much concerned with the politics of expression as with the virtue of Creole and its resourcefulness in conveying certain experiences. In *Slave Song* I talk about the brokenness of the language, and in the brokenness of the language resides not just a certain barbaric energy, but also the capacity to be experimental with a language; it is almost like using Shakespearean English. You can make up words, play with words, and you can rhyme in much more adventurous ways than you can in Standard English. The brokenness has a capacity to convey a greater sense of tragedy and pain, of energy, but you can also reconstruct it in your own way, you can play with the language with a greater degree of freedom. So Creole has its own native strengths and you can convey certain experiences very powerfully in a way that English could not be used. One of its difficulties is that you cannot really achieve a certain level of abstraction in Creole; ideas always have to be conveyed sensuously. So, therefore, you cannot have the *Four Quartets* in Creole, and Eliot on the other hand could not write some of our poems in his language. There is a kind of crudity in Creole – and my use of it was influenced not by living in a village in Guyana, but by being in a library in Cambridge where I was reading medieval alliterative verse, *Piers Plowman*, *Sir Gawain*, and the medieval secular literature which was immersed in all kinds of obscenities and mischiefs. I discovered while being in Cambridge that medieval alliterative expression was beautifully barbaric, and this provoked memory of my native Creole, its 'thew and sinew', its savage energy, its capacity for a savage lyricism.

WB *Your second book, 'Coolie Odyssey', came out four years after the first one, in 1988, and there is hardly any use of the Creole, is there?*

DD There is. In *Slave Song* the Creole I wrote was very close to actual words used in a particular village in Guyana. In *Coolie Odyssey*, although it looks like Standard English, I think that the rhythm of the line and the sound of the poem is Caribbean. So that although I use an English diction overwhelmingly, the Caribbean rhythm of the line and the sound of the poem comes out in the speaking or the reading voice.

WB *Derek Walcott says the same thing. He uses the whole English and the world tradition in poetry and yet his work is unmistakably Caribbean. Let me pick out some poems from this collection. The first poem in the book, which is also the title poem, you dedicated to your grandmother, whom you call 'Ma'.*

DD Grandmothers are so crucial: the whole of Caribbean literature is littered with dead grandmothers, and this was my dead grandmother coming into Caribbean literature. When we left the small town of New Amsterdam to go and hide in the village during the disturbances in '62, it was to our grandmother that we went. The grandmother was a kind of rural protector, nurse, folk wisdom, and folk strength, or we recreate her thus years after the event, when we are far away in England or North America.

WB *Could you comment on the last stanza of the same poem? I assume your mentioning of the "congregations of the educated/sipping wine, attentive between courses" has caused a certain degree of embarrassment among your public.*

DD Yes, the stanza is intended to dampen applause after I have read the poem. This poem was saying, "Look, I have a grandmother, and she is a 'folk' grandmother, and she is dead and I want to write about her". I cannot write about her in the way the Irish, like Heaney, would write about their folk. And I cannot write about her the way Tony Harrison in Britain would write about folk in the north of England. My folk is not like their folk, and there is nothing romantic or snug about my folk; they don't wear cloth caps and don't smoke clay pipes. There is nothing I could romanticize about. I cannot have nostalgia about my folk because they were born in dread and poverty. Nevertheless, I want to find the narratives; I want to find the "folksiness" in my folk. There is a dialogue going on between myself and my dead grandmother, where she says to me: "You are just being stupid; you are just educated. We are not like texts waiting to be written by the children. We are dead and gone like dog bone and dry well. We are nothing". But I still remain before the grave seeking fables. So a kind of dialogue goes on between the dead and the living. And the Whites come in, for I feel I have to write about these experiences – for them. Because I live in England, they will buy and read my poetry expecting "folksiness", expecting maybe exotic things and a display of suffering, or an archive of one's victimization. They will consume all that, and at the end of the day you are left with a dead grandmother and yourself, and a useless poem. I am saying that it is almost a pity one has to write at all. I am almost saying that an immigrant in Britain lacks genuine audience. What is your audience? You don't have an audience in Guyana because you have moved away and are reconstructing Guyana fictionally, perhaps falsely, because of your absence from the place. You are forced to address the Whites, and you address them on issues that have to do with dispossession, and they are such personal experiences that to have the Whites consume them is painful and shameful. It is almost like saying, "I am naked before you".

WB *Another poem I would like you to comment on is 'Miranda'.*

DD Many poems in *Coolie Odyssey* deal with the Miranda-Caliban relationship. That configuration is one that afflicts the Caribbean imagination. West Indian writers have had to rewrite and to respond to the Caliban myth and the Crusoe myth. We had to do that almost as a rite of passage. And in *Coolie Odyssey* I personalize, I individualize these myths and show how they affect me personally.

WB *You are among those who change these myths?*

DD We don't just respond to them. In responding to them, you rewrite English literature. You are being iconoclastic in a real sense, because you know what the icons are, and you know what the mythic structures are. And by shattering them in your personal way, you not only shatter them, you can also alter them profoundly. So it may be that Miranda becomes a whore, or else she becomes the virgin who lusts after our dark skins and tropical experiences, or whatever.

WB *Miranda is less used by Caribbean writers; Caliban is almost a topos in Caribbean literature by now. Do you curse the master with his own tongue?*

DD No. I don't think it is sufficient just to curse the master with his own tongue; it would mean you are not progressing beyond retaliation, reaction. I think what you have to do is revise the myths in a creative way, and in so doing perhaps reveal hidden or original layers of meaning. In other words, it is not sufficient to rape Miranda, because rape is destructive. It is better to love her, the sexual romance peopling the isles with new Prosperos. Better still would be to forget the symbolic designations altogether and respond to men and women according to their contemporary individualities... to call them by their own names.

WB *Would you say that the literary presence of West Indians in the British Isles can be seen in all modesty as an invigorating force of British literature?*

DD Yes. England is now the third largest West Indian island. There are about a million of us, so England is very West Indian. In terms of invigorating contemporary English literature, I have no doubt that the West Indians have rejuvenated the English tongue by using it differently. But also the West Indians have come to England to describe England through West Indian eyes, and therefore they have added startlingly new perspectives on English life and society. Undoubtedly they have added variety to literature in English and a measure of this is the jealousy that the native English writers have had and have for the early and the contemporary West Indian writers. People like Kingsley Amis and John Wain were threatened by the Sam Selvons and George Lammings and the Wilson Harrises. Their reviews of the West Indian novels of the fifties and the sixties were tinged with a kind of contempt that really hid envy.

WB *Who are some of the younger West Indian writers living in England today that you would like to mention?*

DD We have to be grateful to Linton Kwesi Johnson for his early poetry in Creole. He really was a seminal figure in that he was the first poet that I know of in England in this century who had the backing of his community. Linton would head a march of about a hundred people to a police station and would read a poem there about some black man who had been locked up unjustly. And he had the whole community behind him. The community saw Linton as someone who would express things on their behalf. It is almost like the troubadour, the ballad tradition, brought back almost single-handedly to Britain. So he is an important historical figure in English poetry. He gave a lot of us the courage to write as well, because he was catapulted into national fame. Linton influenced a generation of dub poets, Martin Glynn, Desmond Johnson, and others. But parallel to Linton's poetry was the poetry of John Agard and Fred D'Aiguar who wrote in a Creole located in the Guyanese landscape rather than in a black British context. Then you had the emergence of women poets, people like Grace Nichols, who came to national prominence by winning the Commonwealth Prize in 1983. What is exciting for me is that I know all these people personally: we are friends, we read together, and I feel that I am part – however small –of a beginning of a very exciting period in English literature that hopefully one day will be looked back on as an historic era in the development of English literature.

WB *What are the publishing houses for West Indian writers in Britain today?*

DD The "mainstream" presses will take up one or two token black poets. Each of the establishment presses has one. What I find obnoxious or dangerous is the selection of that writer. The commercial presses will select a black writer whose verse does not in anyway threaten or subvert, or tend towards disturbance. They will pick up what I call a "house nigger" poet, one who is willing to imitate English poesy, one whose Creole lacks a kind of barbaric or a vicious edge. In other words, he will be the safe poet, or so they believe. More fool them. Poetry these days is best published either by yourself or with a small press, and there is a proliferation of small, independent presses in Britain.

WB *Could you name a few?*

DD There is Dangaroo Press; there is Bogle L'Ouverture, which is set up by Jessica Huntley; there is New Beacon Press, there is Akira Press; there is Karia Press. These are all black presses run and owned by black people. There must be about twenty black presses in Britain today, and many only produce one or two books a year. Some are badly produced because of a lack of editorial experience, the lack of money to use good illustrations and good paper. But the very roughness of some of these publications is symbolically important. They are saying: "We do not use good quality paper to impress. The word will remain irrespective of the quality of the paper we use". Nevertheless, these presses remain relatively powerless because they have little or no access to the media (which is dominated and influenced by a handful of establishment presses) so their books rarely get reviewed or noticed. Meanwhile, an enormous amount of well-crafted, laminated dross written by select Whites receives attention in the literary journals and book pages of the newspapers. Our one mischievous consolation is that time will tell, and that these contemporary Colley Cibbers will prove to be as ephemeral as the journals which promote their work.

CHAPTER XI

INTERVIEW WITH DAVID DABYDEEN,
1991

FRANK BIRBALSINGH

David Dabydeen's first novel, *The Intended*, was published by
Secker & Warburg in February 1991. Frank Birbalsingh interviewed David Dabydeen prior to the publication of the novel.

FB *I always found it puzzling that you came to England so
    young.*

DD I came in the migration from the West Indies to Britain in
    the 1960s. I was born in Berbice, Guyana, and grew up sur-
    rounded by half eclipsed memories of India that were gained
    through watching films or through observation as a boy of
    Hindu rituals. I was also fascinated by the fact that every
    three months or so some pandit would come along to bless
    something or other. I remember, we had moved to the town of
    New Amsterdam which was largely Afro-Guyanese, and rela-
    tions between them and Indo-Guyanese were cordial and
    normal, apart from the normal biases and innocuous preju-
    dices which operate on a day-to-day level. I went to school
    in New Amsterdam. But, in the 1960s I remember all of us
    had to move from New Amsterdam, back to our Indian envi-
    ronment, because of race riots. I remember all of us packing
    up everything that we had in New Amsterdam and getting on
    a bus and going back to the Indian villages in rural Berbice.

FB *How old were you then?*

DD I was about seven or eight. I was very conscious of being surrounded by our belongings, of people whispering and being afraid of what would happen to them. These were Indian people, getting on the bus and arriving in a village and spending three months there. In other words, one's nascent sense of Indianness was intensified by this experience of racial hostility. It didn't mean that I could speak a word of Hindi, although my grandmother and my great grandmother could. The whole environment was one of cows and wooden houses propped on stilts, and agricultural patterns of living. My uncle used to live in a mud hut, and owned a couple of cows and sheep. People dressed with malas on their heads and big silver bracelets. They were barefooted. This was my sense of Indianness, and it was intensified and contradicted by watching Bombay movies. We thought of India then as being glorious, full of wealth and opulence, of people and palaces, instead of mud huts.

FB *Where exactly was your village?*

DD It was a village called Brighton, on the Corentyne coast. We stayed there for about three months until the riots were over. Then we went back to New Amsterdam. There was always constant journeying back to Brighton village. Every three months, during the short holidays, we went back to Brighton village – that's where most of my family were. In the Caribbean you always return to your grandmother's house.

FB *How long were you at school in New Amsterdam?*

DD Until I was about ten. Then I got a scholarship to Queen's College, Georgetown, the capital city. I was there for about two years.

FB *Did you have family in Georgetown?*

DD No, I boarded with people. This was a very important experience for me. There was a very bright Indian boy called

Bacchus who was my very good friend in New Amsterdam. We both got scholarships to Queen's College, and went off to Georgetown and boarded separately; but bright as he was, he could not afford to live in Georgetown, and had to give up the scholarship. That disappointment demolished him. About four years later he had a chance to emigrate illegally. He went to Canada to start a new life, but someone reported him and he had to go back home. When I saw him five years ago in Guyana, he had turned Christian. After preliminary greetings he said: 'Are you saved?' That question meant that our whole boyhood had disappeared: because of poverty, migration, and the racism in Guyanese society. Although his family were Muslim, he grasped the last straw left to him which was evangelical Christianity. He even joined the People's National Congress which ruled and ruined Guyana continuously for twenty-six years.

FB *When and how did you come to England?*

DD In 1969. My father had separated from my mother and he came to England to make his fortune, as many other West Indians had done. When he made sufficient of his fortune, he sent for us. An elder sister came, then me, and then a younger sister.

FB *Then you went to school here, and on to Cambridge University?*

DD Yes. I went to Cambridge.

FB *And then you went to do a Ph.D at London University in 18th century literature and art. You were also a post-doctoral Fellow at Oxford, and I believe Yale?*

DD Yes, I spent three years at Oxford and a brief time at Yale.

FB *Where does your writing come in? What are the beginnings?*

DD There were two people who were very influential in my writing career. One is an old black man called Mr Spencer, who was headmaster in my primary school in New Amsterdam. He was really important to me in terms of wanting to achieve things. He had been abroad and he would tell us stories of how things were done abroad. So at a very early age he planted in my mind the idea that I had to go abroad to see how things were done. He pushed me, as he pushed many others to scholarships etc. Then the person who taught me at Queen's College – John Rickford, who is now a Professor at Stanford University. He was the head boy, and he got a scholarship to America to do his degree. He was such a brilliant debater and a wonderful teacher. He made us set up a newspaper with stencils to type, and he gave us stories to write. If we wrote a good story or poem, he would let us read it out in front of the class. So he was an extremely creative teacher who inspired us all to write. He had asked us to write a story about a day in the life of a frog, and I had written one of the nicest stories. He read it out to the class. That gave me an audience for the first time, and the pleasure has stayed with me.

FB   *Those were the two main influences in your life, that you can recall?*

DD   The most important influence of all was my whole family – who saw education as absolutely important and urged me to achieve. I was lucky in that one of my uncles had already gone to Oxford – straight from the bush. He grew up in Brighton village, went to school there, then to Berbice High School, where he got a scholarship to Queen's College. He did his 'A' levels and went on to the University of the West Indies where he got a first-class honours in History. This was all in the late '50s, early '60s. He then went on to study for his doctorate at Oxford. So there was already someone in the family who had ventured out, all the way from Brighton village to Oxford. Therefore, I grew up under that influence all the time. Uncle Raja was a little god figure to us. So apart from the outsiders there was also the importance of education in the family.

FB *You felt inspired by the memory of your uncle having achieved things.*

DD Yes. When I went back in 1976 to Brighton village, I saw some of the books that he read for 'A' levels, when he was seventeen, for example, Lionel Trilling's *The Liberal Imagination*. I was in my second year at Cambridge before I came across Trilling. Guyanese of this time were far more advanced than we were. What rather saddens me is that under this PNC Government that we have had for so long, although we had the reputation of being the intellectuals and writers of the Caribbean, we Guyanese are statistically at the very bottom of all the examination leagues in the Caribbean. That is the greatest indictment against the PNC government: they have not just impoverished the people economically, they have impoverished their capacity for expression.

FB *Is 'Slave Song' your first book? I assume by that time you had already written your Ph.D. thesis.*

DD No, I hadn't written my thesis then. *Slave Song* was written when I was at Cambridge. I was about twenty-two, still an undergraduate. It was published six years later in 1984.

FB *When you say 'written' do you mean in the form in which it finally appeared?*

DD I had written four of five of the poems in *Slave Song* while I was an undergraduate at Cambridge. Whilst I was an undergraduate I had the chance to return home. It had been about ten years since I had been home. Leaving as a boy and going back as an adult was probably the most creative process that I've been through. I spent three months at home as an adult, and I had gone back with an apparatus of texts. I had also gone back with Western modes of behaviour as well as modes of reading, and I think the tension between the home environment and the Cambridge environment just created poetry. I immersed myself in that atmosphere for three months, and I found that going back to Cambridge released an enormous amount of creative energy. It reminds me of what C L R James says about West Indians: we have the privilege of being insiders as regards English society, but we are also outsiders. It is the same with our homes, our own villages: we are insiders and also outsiders, and it's that tension of being both insiders and outsiders that makes for excitement.

FB   *Did the poems in 'Slave Song' come in exactly their final form, or were they changed much afterwards?*

DD   They were written in the form that they are at the moment, but obviously they were revised and shaped as they were being written.

FB   *And what about the notes that followed?*

DD   I thought of three things in writing an extensive introduction and a series of notes: it was a literary joke – hence I referred twice in *Slave Song* to T S Eliot, because Eliot had also joked and provided a kind of spoof gloss to *The Waste Land*. On another level, we had been arguing for a long time that Creole was a distinctive language. We made a lot of politics out of that. It was part of the nationalism in the 60s. We had our own airline, environment, landscape, and fruits, so we should have our own language. If we were going to take that seriously we should provide translations to our poems. But the third reason is the most serious. I wanted to write in a minimalist fashion, and I wanted to question the relationship between the work of art and the critical industry that arises because of that work of art. In other words, I was being the critic and the artist together in one book. It was in the '70s when I went to Cambridge that modern critical theory – structuralism and deconstruction – was taking root. Art was being eclipsed altogether. Therefore I was engaged in that whole Cambridge mood where the artist was being eclipsed and the critic became rewriter of art. That book came out of the intellectual environment of Cambridge; but it was also obviously nourished by the Guyanese imagination. It was a deliberately conscious work of literary criticism. It posed the question, which is so central now with Derrida and others, as to the relationship between the artist and the critic, the creative work and the critical work.

FB　*What do you think would have happened if those notes and translations were not there?*

DD　I think the notes and translations take the poems into the realms of prose – very fine, elegant English prose. This throws up questions about the relationship between the prosaic nature of the English language and the intense, rhythmic nature of Creole. I see *Slave Song* as a whole book. It is the book of poems, but it is also a book with literary criticism in it. I don't see how you can separate the two. I'm glad that Wilson Harris, in his review of the book, actually pointed out that it is the juxtaposition of the prose and poetry that creates an added dimension of excitement. If you like, it's mixed media. You have poetry and paintings. Well this is poetry and literary criticism, with images of art thrown in to create confusion.

FB　*I wonder about matters of audience. Obviously, English readers would respond more warmly to this mixed media presentation because it includes explanation and interpretation, and it is therefore easier to follow. But don't you run the risk of the West Indian reader being put off a little, perhaps even being irritated by the fact that he can understand the Creole language directly, yet he has to face the intrusion of the explanation and interpretation?*

DD　I don't think so for two reasons. I see that Brathwaite, in *X*

Self, has followed me in providing a series of extensive notes even though he has abbreviated them. I think that *Slave Song* did have some small impact. Don't forget that in the eighteenth and nineteenth centuries, this kind of writing was not unusual: you had poetry but also extensive introductions. In Pope's case, for instance, he supplied notes to his already extensive footnotes. Pope's own introduction to his poetry tends to be very detailed, and he also footnoted his own poetry. Now I'm not saying that we have to go back to the eighteenth century. What I'm saying is that it has influenced people like Brathwaite, whether they wish to acknowledge it or not, in terms of how they present their own poetry to the West. More importantly, I do not think that our own people, because we happen to be West Indians, understand our own language, or indeed the nuances, or evocations of our language. Just because you can speak a language doesn't mean you can inhabit it creatively and intellectually. I think West Indians will benefit from the notes, if they benefit at all, or they will benefit as much as the English. The notes leave off from the poems at a certain stage and then they just take off in their own direction. They are little prose pieces by themselves.

FB *I found the sexuality of the poems very interesting. I was particularly interested in what you call 'the erotic energies of the colonial experience'.*

DD Well I think that the Empire has been looked at from the perspective of sociology, history, political economy etcetera; but the Empire was also an enormous erotic project. What I was interested in was bringing to the surface the latent eroticism of the encounter between black and white, because it seemed to me that that would be revealing a relatively unexplored aspect of imperial relations. I know that Vic Reid has written a book on the Mau Mau called *The Leopard* which looked at this matter. But it was sensational. It wasn't playful enough. What I did with my re-formation of the eroticism of plantation life was in fact to contextualize it in English medieval traditions of romantic expression. So that you get a Creole poem that quotes the ballad tradition of medieval poetry. One has to be playful with the potentiality of eroticism, otherwise one can get into a very ugly and sensational way of writing. So I 'distanced' myself from the eroticism by overlaying the poems with references outside the plantation experience.

FB   *You leave me somewhat confused about the object of this erotic type of writing. As you say, writing about colonialism has traditionally brought out aspects of economic exploitation, and of the enormous physical abuse of slavery, and so on. I am a little confused about the playful treatment of the erotic aspect of writing poetry.*

DD   First of all one has to say, the pure delight of writing in Creole about erotic experiences is a very sensuous pursuit. Also, you strip away the surfaces of colonial relations to reveal what takes place at the basest level of human emotions and actions. In the way *Heart of Darkness* ceased being an exploration of a different geography and landscape, and became a Freudian exploration of the energies that people exchange. In other words Africa ceases to be a geographical entity and becomes the territory of the human subconscious. Now that is revealing something else about our colonial relations. I think also that it was linguistically important. I was a bit disappointed in a lot of Creole poetry, including my own and Brathwaite's, because I felt that the poets were largely using the Creole in a social realist manner, without a sense of its psychic energy and disturbing quality. They didn't take the Creole to the very edge of breakdown because they didn't have the themes, and unless you stretch a language to its very limits in the way that Salman Rushdie is stretching the English language at the moment, you cannot see the full potentiality of the language. Now the theme that I had which was eroticism allowed me to adventure with the language and to 'pervert' the language, as opposed to Kamau Brathwaite's desire to 'purify' the language.

FB   *There is tension between Indo- and Afro-West Indians in Guyana and Trinidad. Do you think this tension is represented in the language spoken by either group? Are there significant differences between the Creole of Indo-West Indians and the Creole spoken by Afro-West Indians?*

DD   Brathwaite did make a call a few years back for people to start researching into the Indian contributions to the creolization of language in the Caribbean, because all the research is really about the survival of African retentions, and I would hope that what *Slave Song* does is to show how Indian the Creole is, not just in the use of Indian diction – there are many Indian words like 'chamar', 'belna,' 'pookne' – but also in the whole setting of cows, and houses on stilts, and savannahs and paddy fields. That agricultural experience is very Indian, and it is arrogant to marginalize us, to think that we can be on the land, day in and day out, since 1838, and not feel for that land and not belong to that land. You see when you are in the city you don't belong anywhere because you are metropolitan. You are marginal. It is those city-based populations in the West Indies that are the most marginal people. They are the non-West Indians, for they have imbibed all the metropolitan values. We who cut cane and grow rice and get bitten by snakes, are the West Indians who inhabit the spirit of the land, certainly in Guyana. I can't speak for Jamaica and other places where agriculture was sustained by non-Indian traditions.

FB   *Roy Heath has also spoken of the urban experience reducing people to a sameness like other urban experiences. The very title 'Slave Song' encourages me to think about the Afro experience of slavery in the Caribbean, and there are some poems about slavery and master-slave relationships in the book. But the poems which leap at me as most deeply inspired are the Indian poems. I realize that this has come about because of a specific historical context in which African slavery and the plantation system created an environment into which Indo-Caribbean experiences were fitted.*

DD   To describe the Indian experience you really have to start with that parent experience if you like, or you have to acknowledge, or fix it. In other words, what I was trying to do in *Slave Song* was to see a continuum of slave and indenture experience.

FB   *Is it not dangerous to speak of different Caribbean experiences if one set of people suffered more than another set?*

DD   If I am writing about an Indian on a plantation, I will inevitably also convey echoes of the African on the plantation. But if Afro-Caribbean experience is only an echo in my work, it doesn't mean that I am marginalizing the African. It just means that my theme is Indian. There are echoes of Africa always in writing about the Caribbean plantation, but they're becoming more and more inaudible because the African has moved away so far and so fast from plantation life, certainly in Guyana, that the African presence is probably an intellectual memory now.

FB   *When V S Naipaul produced 'A House for Mr Biswas', he was attacked for being ethnocentric, and he defended himself by saying that Trinidad Indian experience was all that he knew. There is not doubt that this experience was conditioned by such factors as displacement, exploitation and alienation, which also influenced Afro-Caribbean experience. But he had to write about what he knew. For this reason, it is not hard to understand why the strength of your inspiration is in your*

Indian-based poems. Perhaps it is for the same reason that I was very impressed by the success of your novel, 'The Intended', in capturing the context of Indian life in the Caribbean. I don't think previous writers have captured quite the same mixture of drunkenness, wife-beating, violence, aspiration and economic cunning. Having the access to raw Guyanese Indian experience which you have reproduced so well, are you now to be considered a Black British writer or a West Indian, or a Guyanese Indian writing in England? In passages, for instance, where you interpret the contradictions between Caribbean and British experience, of the person caught in that contradiction – you are superb.

DD   Writers are privileged when they have a variety of sources to draw from, for example, a variety of landscapes that they have lived in, sometimes partially, or in a variety of languages they have spoken, even though they may overlap, like Creole and English. Writers are absolutely privileged to have this kind of plural, complex, contradictory, background and to be nourished by paradox. So in terms of self-definition I am glad I'm, if you like, a three of four-footed creature, a kind of latter day Anancy as many West Indians are, a spider figure with certainly one foot planted in Africa through my scholarship which was really about the representation of Africans in Western Art and Literature. Intellectually, I have a foot planted in Africa. I certainly have one foot planted in India in an equally ambiguous way, because I can only recapture India in an intellectual way through books, or by visiting Indian friends. Because I am Indo-Guyanese I am already removed from India. And certainly one foot is planted in Europe because, as C L R James says, we are products of Europe, not wholly but partially: we grew up with Shakespeare, we see the English countryside as Naipaul does in *The Enigma of Arrival*, through the lens of Constable and Wordsworth. We can't just have a direct relationship with the English countryside. We must see it through the literary or visual text. So we've got a foot planted in Europe, and then we have a foot planted in our own society, Guyana, and Guyana has its own foot planted in South America. So it is potentially an endless series of poetic feet, landscapes, modes of feeling and thinking, and experiences that are available to us. We should see it as such a privilege. Instead, we see it as a grievance. Historically, some West Indians have said 'Oh God, why can't we go back to Africa? Why can't we go back to India?' To me that is a negation of the imagination, or the sign of an impoverished imagination, an atavistic impulse. It is refusing to see that we are modern people in the sense of having the potential for living in complex states. But we refuse to be complex. This is why in England we set up silly little political parties, or we fall back on narrow nationalisms like the Montserrat Association, the Barbados Association, the Trinidad Association. We are either terrified by our complexities or we turn them into a source of grievance.

FB   *Historically, they have been a source of grievance.*

DD   I think they have been a source of grievance, but I also think that paradoxically the middle passage was profoundly creative. It wasn't meant to be creative, but by removing the African and Indian from home it set up all kinds of tensions. Diaspora set up all kinds of tensions and possibilities for growth. The middle passage was creative, by liberating the imagination from home. Writers have to live outside before they can write about inside; you need that distance. The middle passage gave us a distance from Africa and India. But also it liberated us physically as well. I lost all sense of caste affiliation. I would not have lost that if the British had not moved us to the Caribbean. I would have been possibly a peasant labouring under one of the most oppressive systems on earth, which is the caste system.

FB *You lost your caste but you also lost your language.*

DD We lost our language, and it is an irreparable loss. It's a very felt loss to me. I've always wanted to learn Hindi or Urdu. But you have to take what you have.

FB *I accept that the complexity of the Caribbean experience may include certain benefits. But living here in England as an Indian-looking person, without an Indian language, are you not at a disadvantage when you are subjected to racism for example? Would it not be an advantage to have a language other than English to express your difference?*

DD Yes, but I think I can try to express my difference using the English language. All I'm saying is that if I had Hindi with the same fluency that I have English, then I would have felt more strengthened, more whole. But possibly even more boxed in, because in a sense only having the English language to express my difference means that I will have to be so fantastically creative with the English language. I will have to do things with the English language that maybe it doesn't have the 'natural' capacity for. The English language does not readily allow me to express my Guyanese experience. I have to force the weight of my experience on it and therefore modify the language. New challenges arise out of being trapped in mono-language and having to express differences in it. That in itself creates wonderful tensions that can be exploited by the writer.

FB *You're speaking of literary advantages.*

DD Yes, but I see myself as having the protection of a creative imagination. I draw a distinction between the artist and the immigrant. If I didn't have art, then I would be an immigrant, and I would have nothing to console me in this society which, as you say, is so racist.

FB *You don't live here as an isolated artist, you live among people like yourself: what is your responsibility to these people*

who look like yourself, but don't have the literary advantages
to express themselves creatively in the English language, and
have to go out and suffer from English racism?

DD   But the artist has to go out there and suffer the same. I have
to wait at bus stops, and sit on trains. The Whites don't know
that I am an artist, and they don't necessarily care anyway,
so I am treated like other immigrants in this society, in certain situations, that is. When I speak of the 'protection of the
creative imagination', I mean an awareness of, or confidence
in self, which means you can speak out, or write out. But you
have to see all these things in context. I come from a society,
Guyana, which is as racist and traumatised by race, perhaps
more traumatised than the British society. Even if we argue,
as some historians have, that it was the British who created
racism in the Caribbean, I was born into a racist society, one
in which race was a very important and privileged factor.
Coming here, in fact, for me has been as liberating as it has
been oppressive. There has been a deep liberal mood in
Britain from Magna Carta days to today. The British initiated
and participated in the slave trade. At the same time, aboli-
tion of the slave trade was the first major philanthropic
movement in this country. So whilst there is illiberalism,
there has always been a liberal mood, and we have to exist
in that liberal mood. So I wouldn't dismiss England as a racist society. That is too simplistic. It is racist, but it also has
anti-racist elements, and it is our responsibility as immigrant writers to support, sustain and contribute to the anti-
racist elements, by helping to develop the society as a
whole, and by contributing our arts and sciences, education
and business skills and whatever else to the society; for this
is our home, unfortunately.

FB   *So the future is here?*

DD   There is no other future – the discernable future is in Britain. This is home now, and we have to make it home. I am

not arguing for indiscriminate integration, or for loss of the cultural baggage that we brought with us to this country. What I am arguing for is our contribution to all aspects of society, even bearing with us a sense of our difference. And I do believe that England is spacious enough to tolerate difference in the society; it is big enough to want difference. In the West Indies, in those tiny little islands, if you are different you are a lunatic; you are ostracized, and called an artist or a madman. That is why Naipaul's fiction is so full of different people called 'mad'. In this society you have greater allowance to be 'mad'. When we riot in England, sometimes for very good reason, it is also a refusal to contribute to society. Riots are as negative as they are inevitable.

FB *That's realistic. Whatever the colonial past, it has happened already. People who have come here must accommodate themselves to conditions here. I agree with you. And whereas I am aware of racism in this society, I think you are right to acknowledge anti-racist and liberal elements working against it.*

DD I also agree with E P Thompson who said that there have always been common decencies operating between people in England. People might be racist in a philosophical or abstract sense. They might talk about Pakis in the abstract sense, but if they sit down side by side in a bus, or if they encounter a Paki in the street, in some personal way, the racism diminishes, it is not as intense or as overt as you might think it would be.

FB *I agree these prejudices stem from an intellectual dislike produced by historical factors which are themselves the product of narrow and ignorant attitudes about other cultures. There is the commitment to the normal, social exchanges.*

DD That's at one level. At another level this is a society of books. It's a textual and artistic society. It's a contradiction to say that a society of books is a society of hatred: it has its hatreds, but it also has its books.

FB *You sound like V S Naipaul in the early days when he first came to England and encountered civilized social decencies which he had not experienced at home in Trinidad.*

DD I wouldn't say that I never experienced it at home, because I've experienced great acts of generosity in both societies.

FB *But the generosity at home is more personal.*

DD Yes, it is more personal and family-based whereas the generosity here is more social. We just have to have the confidence and courage to keep saying that this is our society, even if a lot of white people say it is not. We must keep saying it is our society, and believing it not only in the abstract, but in the way that the Indians and Asians coming from Uganda and Kenya in the 60s with all the 'disadvantages' of an alien language, alien foods and ways of dressing nevertheless made enormous waves in the cities, and created businesses that are now major employers in Britain. We West Indians can learn from the Asians. It seems to me a tragedy that Indians have become alienated in the West Indies. What Indians did to the Caribbean was quite revolutionary. In spite of conditions of indenture they brought a sense of voluntary labour, the feeling that labour gains rewards. Up to 1838 labour did not bring rewards in the West Indies, because the people were enslaved. We brought back the work ethic into the West Indies. Why is it that we don't have a major publishing house in the West Indies? That shows you how impoverished we are as a region. So there's an ambiguity in West Indians attacking England. We ourselves can be incomplete, certainly in Guyana's case. We don't even have our own publishing house to give expression to our writers and teachers. It is because we spend our money on our army as a way of stemming the political fury, that we are so backward and incompetent. We have messed up our own society. It's not enough to blame the white man for messing up our society. He may have introduced the elements of mess, but we completed the job with superb finality. That is why everyone in Guyana wants to leave.

FB *In defence, I can say that, in the twenty-five years or so since the white man formally left, the structures of colonialism have remained in place in social and economic terms.*

DD All over the Caribbean we had the middle-classes inhabiting positions that the white man had vacated, and behaving just like the white man at his worst. I think that the scholarship of Clive Thomas and other economic analysts in the region shows that we lost economic markets, not because these markets were dominated by the West, but because we didn't have the capacity to fulfil them. LOME under the EC convention guarantees that they will purchase our sugar. But we cannot produce that sugar. Why? Because of administrative and ultimately political incompetence.

FB *Let us get back to literature, and your novel 'The Intended'. I think it is a very successful novel with much love, sex, and everything. It has an authentic sense of Guyanese life. But how does the structure work? Is there a pattern or significance in the relationship of the Guyanese sections and the English ones?*

DD The narrative structure of the novel has no focal point. It's an unstable narrative. I think that one has to exploit the creativity inherent in creolization, by which I mean that there is a confusion of the past, present and future tenses in the Creole language, and I wanted to exploit the space that that confusion offers. So there is no linear narrative in the novel, even though there is a certain direction to the constant flashbacks and flashforwards. Now that flashback and flashforward are related to one's linguistic condition – the

Creole with its confused tenses. I also wanted to convey the immigrant experience which is not linear, because immigrants are liable to appear and disappear. This is what migrant life is: you appear in one society, then you disappear; you are either deported or move on somewhere else; you are always moving on. That's the structure. It's set on buses and trains, and there is a lot of waiting at bus-stops, a constant sense of travelling which ends up with a boy waiting for a taxi. There are taxis, buses, planes and trains which represent the constant affliction as well as the creative potential of migration or diaspora. So there is a kind of intellectual migration going on as well. The main character migrates to England, but in England he migrates away from his friends.

FB *You have a very good passage on that. I think it was the hero reflecting on the British security and his insecurity, and the mixture of feelings that produces.*

DD I didn't want to get involved in the parade of grievances. One of the old themes in West Indian literature is the crisis of identity. I have a multiple identity. There is no crisis. There is a kind of delight as well as a kind of an anguish in jumping from one identity to the next. It's like electrons which have their own energization circles. Sometimes they jump from one to the next and release an enormous amount of energy; then they jump back to another circle: little electrons jumping. That is not a crisis. That is a delight and poignancy, and hopefully a release of energy. To see it as a crisis would be to invest in historical grievances. To call myself black, and to hate the white is to get back to manichean systems of operating in the world. It seems to me that our West Indian writers have invested too heavily in the monolith of 'the folk'. This is not true for Wilson Harris and V S Naipaul who came from different positions, one cynical and the other Blakean, yet both making the West Indian feel that he is on the threshold of some capacity.

FB *It is interesting that the names of Naipaul and Harris have recurred throughout this interview. But Harris can be so remote. His writing is not very accessible. How is it that he is so influential?*

DD I think Harris's ideas are very stubborn, and ideas have to be converted into art. Lawrence said that the business of the novelist is to reconcile his metaphysics with his actual sense of living. I think that Harris does this brilliantly at times when you get the most sensuous passages about Guyana and Guyanese landscape. But then sometimes, there is the sudden loss of that sensuousness and there is a struggle for the formulation of philosophical ideas which ought to belong in an essay rather than a work of art. I think that when he succeeds there is nothing like it in West Indian literature. There are sudden ideas which emerge out of what he calls a half eclipse. In the middle of the novel an idea will surface, or a few sentences will be thrown up which will suddenly open up a whole new way of seeing things. These fantastic illuminations always come with Harris. The prose is always being illuminated although it is so dark and dense at times.

FB *We used to talk about the fragmentation of colonialism and now this is being interpreted in a more positive way as multiplicity. It is as if the old fragments can now nourish each other in loose association rather than remain broken or useless as in the previous interpretation. Does Harris's work reflect this positive interpretation of multiplicity? Was that there from the very first book 'Palace of the Peacock'?*

DD I think Harris has seen, in the deepest, most uncanny way, the potential of this fragmentation or multiplicity. All his novels really are about a kind of quantum imagination, as Michael Gilkes calls it, where there are no physical laws that are rigid. There are no identities which cannot be transferred or modified. This is what he struggles to convey in his novels. Whether he succeeds is another matter. I think he does mostly. All art fails ultimately, or fails at critical times. At least Harris has taken a different position from Naipaul. Naipaul's position strikes me at times as being similar to that of Negritude, in searching for a stable community or a stable set of ideas. The search for stability is always in Naipaul. To me that can show an unwillingness to adventure into realms of anarchy and confusion which is the modern condition, which is why Naipaul always seems so magnificent, so 19th century in the impeccable, chiselled nature of his prose. His writing seems so colonial as opposed to postcolonial. Postcolonial writing is one of confusion. It has thrown up its own literary form of 'magical realism'. Naipaul does not see in the confusion the possibility of a new regrouping of citizenship. He doesn't see in the babel of languages which exist in London, the possibility of a new language emerging or indeed old languages coexisting within the babel. Why does Babel have to fall down? Still, I would agree with Enoch Powell, whose position in politics seems similar to Naipaul's in literature, and I think to Brathwaite's in his poetry, namely that you must have boundaries. All this revelling and confusion can, at one level, mean an enormous loss of the self or self-confidence. In other words, you cannot be cultural unless you have a sense of boundaries. Now Brathwaite drew African boundaries in the Caribbean, and Naipaul shows the terror of an absence of boundaries. Harris, it seems to me, revels in the absence of boundaries, and that can be dangerous. It can mean that you are a dilettante, that you are loose and have no root or attachment or commitment. But I do hope that I can be intensely Guyanese, or intensely Berbician, or English, or European. In other words, one has the possibilities of inhabiting different masks intensely. I'm not just saying, take one mask, put it on, throw it away, then take another one and throw it away.

FB   *This is a protean vision of something being broken and re-
      made constantly, something in which a process of dissolution
      and regeneration is always active.*

DD   The amoeba never breaks it boundaries, it always has a skin,
      a shell. You always have the nucleus of your soul.

FB   *From the very beginning Harris always talked about that sin-
      gularity, that unity within diversity. There is always a nu-
      cleus.*

DD   Sometimes the nucleus shifts within the body of the amoeba,
      but the nucleus is always there, and there is always a skin or
      boundary.

FB   *So that the person is still whole. The self is still whole.*

DD   Lamming sees the skin as a castle of skin. He would see
      colonials constructing their skin out of stone. But stone is
      not fluid. You can either just obey stone or you can crumble
      and destroy it. I prefer to think that the boundary of you skin
      is not immovable or made out of stone. It is something that
      you have to blow trumpets at and smash down like the walls
      of Jericho. It's amoeboid.

CHAPTER XII

INTERVIEW WITH DAVID DABYDEEN
1994

KWAME DAWES

KD   *T S Eliot's poetry is founded upon a certain dispensational philosophy that posits that in order for Europe (core of Western Civilization) to understand its current schizophrenic self, it must return to its primordial origin, its history: "Time present and time past contained in time future..." and all that. Two interesting things are operating here; the first is the metaphor of society as mad and the need to heal that madness, and the second is the place of history in that process of healing. I detect a certain application of that dispensational reasoning in your tendency to return to the slave and indentured labour past of Caribbean people – it is almost as if there is a need to understand that past before the present can be grasped. Is this part of your rationale for returning to the past?*

DD   I think it's a kind of excavation of self. The layers of the self have been buried in a forgetfulness; which is why I like the 'Turner' painting, because it's the black figure who is submerged in the sea, head first, not feet first. My 'Turner' poem ends on a great note of pessimism. When Brathwaite talks about recovering a sense of the West African Anancy by sight of a cobweb, or when anthropologists go peering behind every sage-bush in the Caribbean for evidence of African retentions, I don't find it altogether convincing. The other selves, the ancestral selves, are so buried that they cannot be easily recovered. So, that frees you up, to then say, "I have no past." Now, that's not a glorious freedom, because it's still immersed in a kind of a sorrow over what has been lost. But then you just have to realize that that's the situation. So I kind of misquote Eliot by saying that, yes, time past is time present and future for the European maybe. In England, where I live, the myth of national identity has been one of an unbroken lineage from Magna Carta days to today in terms of the rule of law, say, or the sense that history has been continuous and peaceful with no major fractures (in contrast, say, to the French Revolution). So England's national identity is based on a sense of gradual progress towards fair play and justice. Now, our condition as Caribbeans is a broken one, and the brokenness is all the more intensely felt when we live in a place like England. 'Turner' was a great howl of pessimism about the inability to recover anything meaningful from the past. But it's a kind of howl that is also a release into the future.

KD   *Isn't there, at the same time, this effort – that is you go through 'Turner' still? I mean, part of the process is going through 'Turner' which takes you to that place.*

DD   Yes. Because I tend to write inside out. If you want to write about love, you write about hate. So, the denial of hope at the very end of Turner is contradicted by everything that went on before. A degree of recovery can take place through what Wilson Harris calls "magical processes of intuition". You can intuit the past. So it's not just a matter of scholarly recovery of data, or reading books about philosophy, or whatever. Moments of intuition can actually provoke in you a sense of the past in relation to the present; you know, a little strain of a sitar might awaken something in you, some kind of sorrow or memory. 'Turner', deals with that, but then, it negates it at the end. After all, it's a poem rather than a piece of social or political or philosophical discourse.

KD *Slavery plays a pivotal role in the poem 'Turner' and in many of the poems in 'Slave Song'. The most striking characteristic of this treatment of slavery is not the propensity to list its horrors as it would appear in an abolitionist pamphlet, but to try and salvage the stories of everyday living that one would imagine belonged to the slave experience. The impact of this approach seems to me to be such that it readily allows us to connect the past with the present in a disturbing way. Can you talk a bit about your encounter with the slave past of the Caribbean and how that encounter has impacted upon your own writing?*

DD I encountered the slave past in two ways. One was just by growing up in a kind of plantation environment, where, whilst the African Guyanese no longer cut cane, they are there – in terms of being buried in the cane fields – there are black ghosts, black jumbies. So it's there because it's the cane experience, it's the parent experience. But then also through study. I mean, my academic work has been on the eighteenth century which was the period of enslavement of Africans. So you recover the stories in the way that *Beloved* was triggered off by a story that Toni Morrison read about the killing of little children. I've got to say that why I don't dwell on the suffering is that that would be obvious; it seems to me that the triumph of *Beloved*, is in the way it does what Eliot does, which is to fuse the intellect and the senses with great potency. Eliot described poetry as "the direct sensuous apprehension of thought". In other words, Morrison wasn't being politically correct; she wasn't starting off with a kind of deliberation or with a set of beliefs – these are given, the intentions are given – but it's her ability to create stories around the philosophy that make *Beloved* a work of art, rather than a political tract or a piece of documentation. Morrison is more interested in how she can recreate sensuously the kinds of stories that allow suffering and grief to come through. I like the distinction Seamus Heaney makes between the expression of grief, which is art, and the expression of grievance, which is social/political protest.

KD *One of the obvious dualities that operate in your work entails the combined heritages of the African past and the Indian past. There is a kind of dialectic synthesis that has emerged in your three collections which reflects this synthesis. Your first collection 'Slave Song' explored the African past, while 'Coolie Odyssey', the second, focuses in some detail on the Indian presence in the Caribbean; 'Turner' establishes a synthesis of the two, for while, ostensibly, 'Turner' is about the tossing of an African slave over the sides of a slaver, the mythic framework of the piece includes the rather central figure of Manu, Hindu god of the deluge. The presence of these two heritages is unassuming in 'Turner', as if you are trying to articulate a new mythology of identity that marries both elements. Is this a product of your own 'creolization' as a Guyanese Indian? In this instance, Walcott's "divided to the vein" takes on a peculiar distinct twist...*

DD In the Caribbean we use that term creolization so easily when, in fact, we don't 'creolize'. For example, there is a massive body of Hindu texts that came over in the nineteenth century boats – I speak of the *Ramayana*, the *Mahabarata* and such – which are epic in theme and bulk, and they've been there for a hundred and fifty years, and yet very very few of our Caribbean intellectuals have even looked at these texts. So, how can we say we are creolized? What I am saying about the Indians you can say about the Amerindians and the Chinese. The first book on Chinese history and culture came out last year, a book by Wally Look Lai. The unfortunate thing about all these matters is that it's

up to the different ethnic groups to write their own history
and culture; to me that's outrageous, because that reveals a
kind of a self-apartheid. Walter Rodney in *How Europe Un-
derdeveloped Africa* called upon Indian scholars to investi-
gate African history – he was seeking a realignment of our
perspectives in terms of historiography, at a time of
decolonization when the two great continents, Africa and India, were becoming free; and he's saying, "Well, let's look
at one another now, rather than the gaze always being European or transatlantic". I don't think we've done that in the
Caribbean, and I speak objectively in view of the massive
ignorance that we entertain about our Amerindian, and our
Indian, and our Chinese, and Portuguese heritages. Obviously, we have to correct that, otherwise, how can we boast
about being a tapestry of peoples and cultures? That can
just be rhetoric, and basically, what it would mean is that
we are still offsprings of Britain. We don't talk about
Indianness or Amerindianness because we don't make the
effort to understand those languages and concepts, whereas
we go and read James Joyce, which is more difficult than
any Vedic scripture. So we are, it seems to me, still labouring in mimicry in the Caribbean, which is alright if we acknowledge that we are Naipaul's "mimic men"; if people
just acknowledge it and move on, fair enough. But we don't;
we create this kind of rhetoric of independence when we're
really dependent on British, and increasingly, American
sources. Now, in terms of transfusions of cultures, *Slave
Song* considered something of the African experience, or
rather experiences (because you don't want to be monolithic
about it). But the African experiences are fictions because
I'm writing intuitively. (Plus I'm living in the twentieth century in a position of privilege; nobody ever beat me, I never
cut cane, I don't know the weight of a cutlass). *Slave Song*
was an Indian book as well because the agricultural envi-

ronment is Indian. If you talk about planting and reaping you're talking about an Indo-Caribbean activity, in Guyana anyway. So you can't write about planting or anything agricultural, even with an African theme, without the Indianness inevitably and unconsciously fusing into that African body of experience. So these fusions are not necessarily conscious acts, they just are. With 'Turner' I didn't know what I was doing with Manu. Manu was a total accident. It was just a name I'd plucked out from memory. And it wasn't until the book was reviewed in *The New Statesman* by an English scholar who edited the *Penguin Book of Caribbean Verse* [Paula Burnett] and identified Manu as the Noah of Indian myth, that I went to my encyclopedia, my *Encyclopedia Britannica* (!) and checked it out and thought, "What a curious accident!" It reminded me of what Wilson Harris says; that when you write something, it's only in revising it that you get clues to a much deeper meaning or a deeper structure. Now the deeper sense of Indianness did not reside with Manu but in descriptions of planting and reaping. Manu was just a kind of trigger, which in some peculiar way forced me to express an Indianness.

KD   *There is at work in 'Turner' both a narrative quality akin to the art of storytelling (I think here of the retrieved memories of the drowning/drowned slave Turner which appear to be set in some mythic landscape) and a complex series of philosophical explorations which echo the poetics of someone like T S Eliot. At the heart of this philosophizing is an unconcealed indictment of slavery and the society that allowed slavery to continue. Was it the narrative instinct – the instinct to "recall the sources of [Turner, the slave's] life" through a reconstruction of his past (through storytelling) that became the engine for the poem, or were you perhaps drawn more to the irony contained in this act of human abuse as caught by Turner the painter? Is it possible to make such a dichotomy, anyway?*

DD Let me say first of all that the Preface which you quote
    from, and all prefaces I've written to everything, including
    Slave Song, Coolie Odyssey, everything, have, in fact, no
    necessary correlation to what goes on in the writing. They
    are, if you like, what makes sense of what you've done.
    Because I really believe, as Walcott does, and definitely as
    R K Narayan does, that (and this isn't getting into
    mysticism or romanticism), the writer can't really explain
    what has been written. In the actual process of writing you
    are feeling your way confusedly towards some kind of
    pattern of meaning. You are trying to order experience in a
    certain way. Nevertheless, you have to write prefaces, and I
    love Aubrey William's preface to the catalogue of one of his
    exhibitions – the Maya Exhibition at the Commonwealth
    Institute in the seventies – when he said, "Look, I'm being
    forced to write a preface, don't believe a word of it or
    believe everything. Take or leave it. I hate having to do it.
    Look at the painting!" In terms of your question, I would
    come back to two things, and maybe this is answering it
    indirectly. First of all, most of the names of animals and
    birds and fish in the poem are fabricated. I just plucked
    them out of my mind one late night whilst writing. The
    desire was twofold: one was to erase recognition of a
    particular landscape, whether India or Africa, and
    secondly, to suggest the possibility of remaking a
    landscape by renaming it, which is of course going against
    the colonial experience. The second thing is that I
    deliberately set the poem in the sea. Most of it takes place
    in the actuality of the sea, and the sea is actual, not just as
    the location of the drowned man, but in the rhythms of the
    poem. The drowned man's landscape is ghostly and part of
    that ghostliness is the fabricated names of the fauna and
    the flora. This is another aspect of creolization: I don't
    want to be 'authentic' about the African experience nor do

I want to be 'authentic' about the Indian experience, because I'm neither; but I'm both in a kind of ghostly way. England has a very concrete sense of its past which is very visible in terms of fortresses and castles and displays of ancient weaponry and statues of men wielding weaponry and monuments to national heroes who were also mass murderers – you know, the 'hero' of the Morant Bay rebellion, the 'hero' of the Indian mutiny; if you killed more than four or five thousand people you got a statue erected in your honour. So if you live in England where the English have a very powerful concrete, (or stone/marble) sense of their histories, and you as a Caribbean person come to a sense that your history is nebulous and shifting, it means that you have a tremendous capacity for a new kind of freedom, which is what Manu was talking about in the poem – he's saying, you can dream, you can surmise, you can invent. The nebulousness of one's background gives one a kind of epistemological freedom, an existential freedom. To me that's what creolization should be; coming to an awareness that we are free; not because it was the British intention to make us free, but in a peculiar way we became free, we were freed of certain traditions, knowledges and so on; and while we have sorrow about the loss of those, nevertheless, we are always on the threshold of originality.

KD *I am fascinated by this act of inventing names for the fruits and birds of the mythic land that you describe in 'Turner'. I am reminded of Brathwaite's fascination with naming in 'The Arrivants', but in his poem, the names are retrieved through a journey back, through a journey to an existing origin which is found, in that instance, in the ancient civilizations of West and North Africa. When things are named again, they are reclaimed. This reclaiming occurs in your poem, but the names are made up. It is as if the amnesia is insurmountable and the Africa that is constructed is mythic*

and defined in terms of the current space of exile. The state-
ment that this makes about Caribbean society and its rela-
tionship to Africa or India is fascinating. In some ways, it
patterns or confirms the ideology of Rastafarianism, for in-
stance. To what extent do you think the process of construct-
ing one's past, even if that past has no resemblance to the
"real" past (whatever that is), important to survival in the
Caribbean?

DD   I'm really pleased that you picked up the Rastafarianness of
the poem's mood. Before 'Turner' I published a novel where I
had a Rastafarian character who is a peculiar character, a
peculiarly intellectual kind of figure – basically he floats,
and the rest of the characters are rooted. It's set in London.
I'm not talking about the Rastafarian as a Rastafarian, but
about the notion of the Rastafarian. Rastafarianism was important as a 'concept' to me because of course there is the
overlap with Hinduism; the smoking of ganja (supplied on
the plantations to the Indians by the British) or all kinds of
other ritual and mystical correspondences. At this stage in
my life I wouldn't mind exploring the possibilities of freedom – freedom being the desire to invent totally, and to live
in a body of myth of one's own invention. There are, I suppose, echoes of Blake, and definitely D H Lawrence – because I grew up on D H Lawrence – who was trying to create
a private myth by which he could exist in a place like England. The idea of art, or the writing of an individual artist,
being ultimately a social death and withdrawal into a self-
mythologizing is fascinating.. What it doesn't mean is an
abandonment of social and political responsibility. In other
words, I am not going to shave my head, grow hairs on my
chest, and sit under the nearest peepal tree and fast unto
death; not just in the Indian way, but, you know, all those
Catholic martyrs living up nut trees and that; I am not going
to do that, because at the end of the day you have to live and

eat and live in a community and your imagination is nurtured by that community. So you'll still write political tracts
or you'll still be a Paki at a bus stop in England, ten thugs
around, and you're still shit-scared because you don't have
enough money for a taxi fare – you don't get away from those
things. But I think in art anyway, I want to explore the possibilities of a total freedom from the social being.

KD   *'Turner' is a departure for you in several respects. On the one
      hand, it is written predominantly, if not entirely, in standard
      English. As well, there is a far more sustained attempt to con-
      tain the poem in a complex of images that play on the sea,
      sailing, ship-lore, drowning, etc, through the use of echoes,
      metaphors and densely fused images:*

      First a woman sobs
      Above the creak of timbers and the cleaving
      Of the sea, sobs from the depths of true
      Hurt and grief, as you will never hear
      But from woman giving birth, belly
      Blown and flapping loose and torn like sails,
      Rough sailors' hands jerking and tugging
      At ropes of veins, to no avail. Blood vessels
      Burst asunder, all below-deck are drowned.

      *Do you see 'Turner' as a watermark for you, the kind of opus
      that represents a technical and intellectual 'arrival' in your
      poetry? I suppose I am struck by the confidence that seems in-
      herent in the perceived voice...*

DD   'Turner' is the only thing that I have written so far which I
      feel comfortable with. I suppose I spent twenty years just
      trying to find an Africanness or find an Indianness or find a
      Creoleness; a kind of constant grind to find something, and
      now you settle for a world of your own making, and you settle
      for metaphor – the sheer beauty and autonomy of the meta-

phor. We live in a world where we are burdened by meaning. In this politically correct world, we are trying to find meaning all the time, and to express that meaning in rational terms. Given the race relations situation in America and the Caribbean or Britain, writers are expected to be very correct, to bear all kinds of responsibilities towards the notion of being 'truthful' and 'moral' and to provide a kind of explanatory system by which people can live. What pisses me off about critics or about community activists (I used to be one of each, in earlier years) is that they expect a consistency from you and they expect a kind of linear development or they expect sense from you all the time; and you have to be 'one of the boys' and you have to be saying the right things on television, and defending the race. It's a very sincere expectation but I think it goes against the nature of the very processes of writing, where you are much more interested in at times is transgression, and abandonment, and the confusion of metaphor, and opaqueness, and multiply-fused yet contradictory perspectives, and revelling in contradictions, muddle, wrong-headedness, hydra-headedness.

KD *Your poetry is filled with 'classical' echoes, poetic echoes from various cultures as if you see your palette as being quite unlimited and unrestricting. Is this how you feel? Your work engages in a certain flattery of other writers in some instances. Walcott's maritime metaphoring in 'Omeros' has some echoes in 'Turner', Brathwaite's rhythm and line breaks are clearly a presence in 'Love Song', and Eliot makes his appearance in 'Turner' along with Shakespeare and Homer, and in other instances, you appear to be taking on these writers, the most obvious being Ruskin's narrative on Turner the painter and your reworking of Shakespeare's Caliban mythos in 'Miranda', 'Caliban', 'Water With Berries', 'Rebel Love' and 'New World Words.' This layering of echoes and references along with internal debates and feuds lends some of your work what ap-*

pears to be an intensity which can be interpreted as elitist or alienating in some contexts. Are you very conscious of all of this as you construct/create?

DD I'm conscious when I write prose of Selvon, Harris, Naipaul, Lamming and others; I'm conscious. In fact in the last novel I did, I used a character from Wilson Harris' *The Secret Ladder*, Fenwick. And I asked Harris. I said, "Bwoy, you mind if I... ?" He said, "No, man." And I said, "Well, would I go overboard if I take a quote from *The Secret Ladder* and use it as an epigraph?" He said, "No man. Go!" And then I used a character called Jack from Naipaul's *Enigma of Arrival*. And Selvon is everywhere in terms of a certain peasantry and boyhood, growing up in an Indian environment. Lamming is there when I talk about Miranda and Caliban. I'm thinking of Lamming's *Water With Berries* and *Pleasures of Exile*. I suppose, when I look back at it, what I'm trying to do is to say that whereas our writers had to rewrite the 'masterscripts' of Europe, my interest now, from another generation, is to rewrite or respond to our ancestral writers (who, incidentally, are all male – Brathwaite, Selvon, Harris etc – since the Literature of the 40s to the 60s was overwhelmingly by males. No-one knew of Rajkumari Singh or Louise Bennett until very very recently). So my particular interest now is fuck the 'master-scripts', let me write instead to Harris and to Naipaul, write back, quarrel with, borrow from, love, praise, worship them. So, if there is a certain kind of eclecticism, it is not a knee-jerk response to western texts. The other thing is that all these writers are living, and they've helped me. Wilson Harris said, "Give up criticism, go and write poetry." Aubrey Williams provided paintings for my front covers. Sam Selvon – he and I would go and drink and smoke and behave bad. They are a very living presence, these older figures. Sometimes I feel though that I am an allusion to an allusion to an allusion. I'm like one of Eliot's footnotes. I'm just a footnote to an Eliot poem which is in turn a footnote to other writings by other peoples. That's part of the idea of disappearing – there is no fixity, there is no structure; in my head are just echoes of everything. What I am in myself, in essence, I don't know. I'm living in Britain, I'm not living in the Caribbean. If I were living in the Caribbean, I'd probably turn out, hopefully, like Lovelace, who is rooted in landscape and communities. Eliot is modernism, Eliot is fragmentation, Eliot is the disembodied consciousness. Eliot is the great escape artist, Eliot is Anancy in the way that he escapes from Victorian verse, from meaning or from epistemologies, and in a peculiar sense Eliot is the parent of Caribbean poetry. Isn't that peculiar? A racist, conservative, anglo-loving fucker like him, right! But these are some of the beautiful ironies of literature.

KD *All this brings us to the question of audience and your understanding of who your audience is as you write. Is it important to you to have a clear sense of your audience? Being a resident of Britain yet working with a clear Caribbean focus, what kinds of challenges do you face with regards the question, "who are you writing for?" Jean Breeze, for instance, has said that she writes to a black audience – anyone else who happens to hear is overhearing. She welcomes the eavesdropping but she does not plan to do the work of explaining what she means for them. It is an interesting perspective...*

DD The business of writing is so blasted difficult and takes so long and takes so much out of your life and gives you so much, that believe me, you haven't got time for 'audience'. You just want to write the fucker on the paper. After it's finished, the question of 'audience' comes in. The audience I seek are people like Wilson Harris. I'm scared of George Lamming, and I'm scared of Wilson Harris. Now that Aubrey Williams is dead, I'm no longer scared of him except in a kind of jumbie way. These are the people to whom you have

a responsibility, and I feel that very consciously. I was so
torn when I heard rumours that Brathwaite didn't like *Slave
Song*. If fifty thousand others didn't like it and fifty thousand
others liked it, it was Brathwaite that I was scared of. When
I would see Selvon, I used to say, "Yuh know Sam, man, I'm
trying to hustle a bit of fiction here to give you a bit of competition; wha' yuh think of it?" And he would say, "Don't
worry, you know... " Those are the people I clear my work
with. Whether the English understand it or not, whether they
are white or black, I don't worry about those things too
much, because one realizes that art is so private at times
that nobody will understand it, anyway. Secondly, every time
you utter you're open to misinterpretation; some creative,
and some wilfully malicious. I haven't got a romantic view of
black audiences or West Indian audiences. I move with 'the
boys,' they would eat food with me, they would like the idea
of a book – "the boy writing book" and so on, and they will
always look after you because you are a writer, but they are
not gonna read the stuff; and if they read it some of them
might be offended. The first novel I did was set in a village
in Guyana. I used some of the names of the characters who
were still there. I felt I could do that with members of my
family, but I stupidly took the novel back and the next day,
somebody had flicked through it, and I was really in trouble.
They said, "We didn't like this at all... " I was worried as to
whether they were attacking the themes or the way life was
represented. They were, but they were more offended by the
fact that I used the word "fuck." One man said to me, "Man,
yuh get permission to write 'fuck' in a book?" So I said,
"you know, in Englan' you don' need to." He said, "Still,
man, why yuh use 'fuck', why yuh don' say something else; it
look so nasty." So that was a really interesting (mis)reading,
but it didn't necessarily teach me anything. And of course,
once you buy the rum, all the differences are forgotten. The

way out of hostile criticism in a Caribbean village is to buy
rum for everybody. I am being flippant, but you know what I
mean. What I mean is that they don't really necessarily care
for the books. They've got their own lives to live. "So alright,
so the boy bring home a book, so what?" It gives you status,
but at the same time it doesn't seem to be anything special
when you are a villager looking after cow and sheep. There
is comedy as well as a pathos in the presence of a 'book' in a
peasant village. I came across the comedy a couple of years
ago when one of the villagers, hearing of my arrival, wan-
dered into the yard where I was drinking with relatives. He
was an uninvited guest, so to secure his share of rum he
came up directly to me and said. "Man I hear you is a writer
and ting. What you think 'bout Dickens, eh? What you think
about Dickens?" And he spent the next four hours asking the
same question, and drinking, until he collapsed in utter in-
ebriation. In other words, Dickens, whom he'd heard about
somewhere and somehow, was suddenly of moment; what was
obscure and irrelevant in his life suddenly became a very
necessary passport to unlimited rum. The pathos I came
across in a conversation with my mother, who, as a peasant-
child in the village, had the job of sweeping her uncle's
house. Although a total alcoholic and utterly self-destruc-
tive, he was rare in having books in his house. This was ex-
traordinary – books in a village-house in 1940's Guyana. My
mother said that one day, some pages fell from a book which
was by an open window. The book's binding was rotten with
age and the tropical weather and the wind blew some pages
from it. She picked one up and it was headed 'Iliad'. She
told me recently, "I hold it up and I read I-L-L-I-A-D and I
wonder, what name so?" Fifty years later she still didn't
know what it was all about, but the triumph of our Caribbean
achievement is that her children – Brathwaite, Walcott,
Kincaid – can not only read, but rewrite Homer.

KD   *In poetry, personal memory can be both a rich source of inspi-*
     ration and material as well as a treacherous task master that
     desires to consume all that you create with sentimentality
     and nostalgia. I am struck by the absence of these qualities in
     your poems that appear to retrieve old memories. But there
     are times when the eschewing of sentimentality creates a
     hardened realism and irony that seems cold and detached.
     How do you contend with these pressures as you try to con-
     struct a sense of your personal past in your poetry?

DD   I like Brathwaite's view of poetry which echoes Eliot's view
     of poetry – which is that poetry is rhythm. And I think
     rhythm creates music that is deeply sensuous. So if your
     theme is utterly bleak or hard or lacking in sentiment, if it's
     done with a kind of rhythmic beauty and with metaphoric
     colour, that helps to assuage the kind of tight-arsed, con-
     servative retreat from life which sometimes you get in
     Naipaul. I mean, I quite like Naipaul's absence of senti-
     ment, but if I have a quarrel with Naipaul, it is that I don't
     like the way that that absence of sentiment is not conveyed
     or expressed with richness of metaphor or generosity of char-
     acter-creating. *King Lear* is fucking bleak, man, nothing is
     more bleak, but look how beautiful it is. So while one es-
     chews sentiment because it creates bad art, I think one has
     got to express bleakness with a generosity of creativity, with
     music and sensuousness, otherwise it's just a dry, tedious
     self-denial.

KD   *Your poem 'For Rohan Babulal Kanhai' is one of the most*
     moving cricket poems from the Caribbean that I have read. I
     suppose it stands on par with Brathwaite's 'Rites'. In your
     poem the centrality of cricket as a way of understanding the
     Caribbean identity is most vividly and touchingly articu-
     lated. Perhaps the most telling image is that of Kanhai in
     some foreign place alone in the middle accumulating centu-
     ries. Can you talk a bit about cricket as a kind of myth-mak-

ing entity, a central idiom in Caribbean society that in many
ways, defines the society and helps to shape that society?

DD   I got to answer that by acknowledging a couple of things that
I've read that helped to provoke that poem. One was a quite
beautiful essay on Rohan Kanhai by a Guyanese scholar
called Clem Seecharan, who grew up as an Indian in the
Indian parts of Guyana and hero-worshipped Kanhai as most
Indians did. And then, I read an exhilarating poem by a
Trinidadian writer called Faustin Charles which connected
up the force of cricket with conquistadorial energies. That's
how the Kanhai poem came about. It's about the West Indian
experience in two ways. One is Kanhai batting lonely in
some far county called Warwickshire which is the West
Indian pioneering moment. We are all pioneers, you can find
us in all corners of the earth; in darkest Russia or darkest
England, there is some West Indian somewhere, doing his
thing. And he's creolizing the thing. And Kanhai created a
sweep shot. CLR James said of Kanhai, he was one of the
few people to create a new stroke in cricket – the sweep
shot. And what CLR was saying was that the boy took on all
the rules and regulations of cricket which is an English
game and he created a shot. In other words, in the same way
we create the steel band or we create a creole. But then, the
sadness of the poem is that that creativity, because of the
barbarism in our own native society at times, that creativity,
instead of being seen and received as the grand feat of
creolization and celebrated as that, becomes the weaponry of
one race against the other. I wanted to reflect the conditions
of Guyana where we broke into ethnic enclaves. Whilst we
had the rhetoric of creolization, we were in fact ethnocized.
So there's a paradox of Kanhai being a creole figure in England but not a creole figure in Guyana. So it comes back to
that question that we started off with: Are we gonna be properly creolized or not? The other thing, of course, is that

cricket is a form of energy that is the same form of energy as
cane cutting, and Carnival. So that you can't separate the activities. It's a metaphor of the transformation of the middle
passage. The root of it is an inventiveness – not just survival; you can survive with a bit of food – but it's the inventing that matters, the inventiveness, in this instance, of the
Guyanese people. What pisses me off most when I meet
Indo-Caribbeans or Afro-Caribbeans – and I don't want to be
innocent here – but they have rabid racial views. In Miami,
an Indo-Caribbean accosted me and said, "Well, you know
all these black people don't understand our Hindu aesthetics
and Jees, we gotta hold on to our... " Yeah, fair enough, I accept all that stuff, but I'm not gonna express or politicize it
in that way. Or else I meet some black guy who says to me
"How come you put Manu in there? Are you blotting out my
African teachers?" And I say, "No, man, it's just there as a
kind of a way of exploring possibilities of being together." So
you always get that kind of shit. But the best thing about the
Kanhai poem is that just as I have always been afraid of
Lamming and Naipaul, I've been afraid of Kanhai, because I
grew up with Kanhai as the great Indian hero in a racially
polarized Guyana. And when I was in Guyana in 1993, I saw
Kanhai in a boat, crossing the Berbice River. And I fumbled
in my suitcase, I really fumbled about in my suitcase because I had taken some books home for people, and books to
leave in the libraries, and I went up to Kanhai very shyly
with *Coolie Odyssey* and the Kanhai poem. I went up to him
and I said, "Excuse me, my name is David Dabydeen and I
teach at the University of Warwick." And he said, "Yeah?"
No recognition, just "Yeah?" That kind of hoggish, plantation response. He said, "Yeah?" So I said, "I'm a writer and
I wrote a poem for you." He said, "Yeah?" And then I
opened up the book to the Kanhai page and he looked at it,
and this is God's truth, he looked at it and he said, "Yuh

spell me name wrong." Not, "By the way, thank you, but the
name is spelt wrongly" He said, just straight out, in a kind
of plantation staccato, "Yuh spell me name wrong." So I
said, "How you mean?" And he said, "Well, middle name, it
get two '1, it get two '1' dere, boy." So I said, "Well, aww, I
didn't know that. In the next edition, I'll get it corrected."
Well he doesn't know what a 'next edition' is, he doesn't
know about editions and all that kind of stuff; and that was
it. He just closed the book and I just walked away sheep-
ishly, thinking, "You coolie bastard!" That total uncouth
coolie. . . I mean, when I say uncouth, it's also the beauty of
the Guyanese; that lack of reverence, that rumshop kind of
wit and readiness in putting you down, which you've got to
admire. And I suppose if you look at it, what I could interpret him as saying is, "How come you spelt my name wrong?
Everybody spells my name wrong. That's why I'm a plantation coolie. They, the whites, spelt our names wrong or
changed our names. You can't spell my name wrong like
that!" What he did not understand, which I couldn't explain
to him, was that I got it from Wisden, the bible of cricket,
the white man's text. So, in a curious sense, to discover his
middle name (Babulall) I had to go through Wisden which
didn't recover his name. All these kinds of ironies. The reception of a poem like that becomes a metaphor of our Caribbean transformation.

KD *The Guyanese landscape is legendary for its influence on the
work of Guyanese writers – that sense of expanse, an understanding of the river as source of sustenance and as enemy.
Your poetry reflects this grounding in the landscape, particularly the dialect poems of 'Slave Song' and 'Coolie Odyssey'.
The Canje River is a constant presence that has the capacity
of assuming mythic proportions. Can you talk a little bit
about the importance of this landscape to your writing? Has
being away from Guyana all these years and living in an-*

other kind of landscape, had an impact on your own sense of place as it emerges in your poetry?

DD I think so. Probably in a variety of ways, but the most obvious way for me is living in England, where the landscape is very tame, you know, the only wildness in England are the human lager louts, but the landscape is very tame and gentle; almost a classically lyrical landscape. It is interesting that whenever Naipaul describes the landscape in *Enigma of Arrival* which is set in the English countryside, he always alludes to Wordsworth and Constable. In other words, living in England, the landscape for me is a literary landscape. And that's partly because we are colonials and we read the literature, so the places have a kind of mythic literary quality. England has been written about, so that everywhere is very alive with literary evocation. The Guyana landscape is terrible and unwritten. It has a terror, the terror of the unwritten. And I don't mean that in a negative sense. The unwritten is terrible because it is unknown. And it also has terrors in real ways. I mean, I can't swim because my mother would prevent me from going to the pond because in the pond lived all kinds of dangerous creatures. And there were alligators, and we grew up with snakes in the countryside and even in the towns. Snakes and alligators, and we were always being stung by malabunters and there was always something there to make you scream, scorpions and centipedes – everybody got bitten by mosquitoes and so on. So living in England really intensifies my sense of the 'frontier' dangerousness of the Guyanese landscape. The other thing, of course, is that I can't live in the English rural landscape. I don't feel committed to England. I mean, I can survive in the English urban setting because a city is a city is a city, but in England a rose is a rose is not a rose. It's not my rose. I don't know the names of birds and trees and flowers and I don't feel as if I'm interested because I don't feel as if I could really get in

there. Migration is too young a process for us to actually
evolve into the landscape and creolize it. So England's landscape then becomes iconic. It is never a real tree, it is always an icon of something else, and that's probably the way
landscape comes into whatever I'm writing. This is why I
like the idea of the sea, you see. The last novel was about
the sea. It was set in the sea off the Hastings coast. The sea
frees one up from landscape. It's the sea, and the idea of being born in the sea and being an Adam in the sea . . . and
dreaming one's own landscape... starting all over again. Imagine it!

KD *Your poems that deal with sexuality and sexual relations appear to be marked by deeply complex interracial tensions
which lead, very often, to a certain impotence or dysfunc-
tional sexuality. This idea of racial disquiet as imaged
through the metaphor of interracial sexuality is at once provocative and deeply pessimistic – in many ways it reminds me
of the peculiar sexual dynamics in Naipaul's 'Mimic Men'.
My question may sound like one about your sexual experience, but it isn't, the problem is simply that you deal with
racial dynamics through the situation of sexual relations. I
am interested in your thoughts on the racial dynamics that
operate for an artist 'of colour' in Britain. Is the racial landscape as festered with aborted foetuses and impotence as your
poems seem to suggest?*

DD It's what's most obvious about what I write; the interconnec-
tion of racial, historical and sexual themes. It's partly autobiographical and partly not autobiographical. I mean, I feel
as if I'm an abortion, at times. I feel like the stillborn child
in 'Turner', definitely. Or even worse than that, I feel like an
abortion; messy and bloody and unborn, and that's partly
because of a racism, where other people are trying to reduce
you to nothing all the time and erase everything that you
brought with you, or else they remind you of what you could

have brought with you had they not taken it away. But it's
also a kind of general human feeling; we all feel deeply pessimistic at times, the greatest emotion is really the sense of
the tragic rather than the sense of the comic, which is why
King Lear is better that any of Shakespeare's comedies. The
tragic sense is what galvanizes all of us. We switch the television on and we see people dying in Rwanda – tragedy is
much more and always with us. So that's partly it. The other
thing is that I suppose I wanted to explore the idea that the
'Empire' was a pornographic project; it wasn't just an economic or a sociological or a political project, it was also a
project of pornography. And Wilson Harris in providing a
blurb for *Coolie Odyssey* talks about the ways the poems reveal the disturbing pornography of Empire. I suppose that's
all I wanted to say, that ultimately, the plantation experience
had severe and traumatic psychic impacts that had to do
with the loss of, or the traumatic changes in epistemologies
and philosophies, but overwhelmingly had to do with what is
the very ground of our being, which is our body. Now, that's
how I've seen it, but believe me, other people don't see it
like that – and thank God, right? Then again, it's always
been easier for me to write the morbid and the tragic than it
is for me to write something else. I don't know why. That's
all there is. I wouldn't want what I write to be a manifesto of
colonial feelings. Yes, it has a dimension of truth, but there
are other truths which should compete with it. There are
deeply autobiographical moments as well. I grew up without
a mother, so that the absent mother is probably what moves
me very deeply and creates writing. 'Turner' is really about
.the absent mother, too. So there are those moments of autobiography. So when one speaks of an abortion, one is also
speaking of the absent mother; the absence is the mother,
not the life in the child. Then there are autobiographical moments that are also related to the disgust that I felt when I

was young in Guyana, at men beating up women. Some of my most painful memories of Guyana are of men beating up women; not just in my own family, but neighbours, and women crying late at night. I was trying to highlight things that moved me for a variety of reasons – certain social experiences, certain family experiences, certain deeply personal experiences that create a mood of, at times, disgust and, at times, bleakness. But I certainly wouldn't want it to be used as a manifesto of black/white relations or male/female relations.

BIBLIOGRAPHY

Books by David Dabydeen

1 *Slave Song* (poetry), Dangaroo Press, 1984.

2 Ed. *The Black Presence in English Literature*, Manchester University Press, 1985.

3 *Hogarth's Blacks: Images of Blacks in Eighteenth Century English Arts*, Dangaroo Press, 1985/Manchester University Press, 1987/Georgia University Press, 1987.

4 *Hogarth, Walpole and Commercial Britain*, Hansib, 1987.

5 Ed. *India in the Caribbean*, Hansib, 1987.

6 *A Reader's Guide to West Indian and Black British Literature*, Hansib, 1988.

7 *Coolie Odyssey* (poetry), Dangaroo Press, 1988.

8 Ed. *A Handbook for Teaching Caribbean Literature*, Heinemann, 1988.

9 *The Intended* (novel), Secker and Warburg, 1991.

10 Ed. *Black Writers in Britain, 1760-1890*, Edinburgh University Press, 1991.

11 *Disappearance* (novel), Secker and Warburg, 1993.

12 *Turner – New and Selected Poetry*, Jonathan Cape, 1994.

13 Ed. *Cheddi Jagan: Selected Speeches 1992-1994*, 1995.

14 *The Counting House* (novel), Jonathan Cape, 1996.

15 Ed. *Across the Dark Waters: Indian Identity in the Caribbean*, Macmillan, 1996.

Articles by David Dabydeen

1 'A Guyanese Experience of England', *Planet*, Spring 1988.

2 'Race and Community in Anglophone Caribbean Literature', *Toronto South Asian Review*, ed. F Birbalsingh, 1986.

3 'The View from the Colonies', in Leslie Smith, ed. *The Making of Britain*, Macmillan, 1987.

4 'On Not Being Milton: Nigger Talk in England Today', in Christopher Ricks, ed. *The State of the Language*, California University Press, 1989; Faber 1990.

5 'Cultural Diversity', in Mark Fisher and Ursula Owen, eds. *Whose Cities?* Penguin, 1991.

Articles, Reviews, Notices of David Dabydeen's Creative Work

1 **Slave Song**:

   Caribbean Times, (London) 30 Nov. 1984; *Contemporary Literary Criticism* (Vol. 34, 1984, pp. 147-150), ed. Sharon K Hall, Gale Research Company, Detroit; *Clio* (Wisconsin, USA), Vol. 15, No.1 1985; *British Book News*, Feb. 1985; *Multicultural Teaching*, Summer 1985; *Commonwealth Currents*, Feb. 1985; *West Africa* (London), 6 Aug. 1985; *Kyk-Over-Al* (Guyana), No. 31, 1985, *Wasifiri*, Vol.1, No. 2, 1985; *Dragon's Teeth*, No.24, Summer 1986; *New Statesman and Society*, 5 Jan. 1990.

2 **Coolie Odyssey:**

   Morning Star, 1 March 1988; *Asian Times* (London), 4 March 1988; *Trinidad Guardian*, 30 March 1988; *West Indian Digest* (London), April 1988; *Poetry Review*, Summer 1988; *The Listener*, 8 Sept. 1988; *Sunday Sun* (Trinidad), 18 Sept. 1988; *The New Bajan* (Barbados), Nov. 1988; *The Independent*, 5 Nov. 1988; *Orbis*, No. 71, Winter 1988; *London Review of*

Books, 20 April 1989; *Third World Quarterly*, Vol. 11, No.4, October 1989; *Contemporary Poets* (ed. T Chevalier, St James Press, London, 1991); *Poetry Review*, Vol. 83, No. 1 and No. 2, Spring and Summer 1993.

3   *The Intended*:

Guardian, 10 April 1991; *Asian Times* (London), 5 Feb. 1991; *The Bookseller*, 8 Feb. 1991; *Observer*, 17 Feb. 1991; *Guardian*, 21 Feb. 1991; *City Limits*, 21 Feb. 1991; *Independent on Sunday*, 24 Feb. 1991; *The Voice*, 26 Feb. 1991; *Time Out*, 27 Feb. 1991; *Daily Post*,28 Feb. 1991; *Times Literary Supplement*, 8 March 1991; *Weekend Telegraph*, 9 March 1991; *The Voice*, 12 March 1991; *Coventry Evening Telegraph*, 16 March 1991; *Sunday Times*, 14 April 1991; *The Advocate* (Barbados), 26 April 1991; *BWA* (Bulletin of the Welsh Academy), No.22, Spring 1991; *Times of Zambia*, 10 May 1991; *Red Letters* No. 29, Summer 1991; *Bazaar*, Summer 1991; *Toronto South Asian Review*, Summer, 1991; *Morning Star*, 3 June 1991; *London Review of Books*, 11 July 1991; *Kunapipi*, Vol. 13, No.5, 1991; *Caribbean Review of Books* (Univ. of West Indies, Jamaica), 4 May 1992; *The Mail on Sunday*, 21 June 1992; *Observer*, 22 Nov. 1992; *Chronicle* (Guyana), 7 Nov. 1992; *Mirror* (Guyana), 13 Dec. 1992; *Planet*, Vol.90, 1992; *Ariel* (Canada), Vol. 24, No.1, 1993; *World Literature Today*, Winter 1993; *The Weekend Review* (Adelaide), 27-28 Feb. 1993.

4   *Disappearance*:

The Guardian, 5 Jan. 1993; *Australian Bookseller and Publishers*, Feb. 1993; *The Observer*, 7 Feb.1993; *Australian Book Review* No. 148, Feb/March 1993; *Tribune*, 4 March 1993; *Midweek* (Australia), 4 March 1993; *Sunday Chronicle* (Guyana), 7 March 1993; *Times Literary Supplement*, 12 March 1993; *Financial Times*, 13 March 1993; *Stabroek News* (Guyana), 2 April 1993; *The Independent*, 24 April 1993; *Morning*

Star, 10 May 1993; *World Literature Today,* Summer 1993; *New Statesman and Society,* June 1993.

5   *Turner:*

The Times, 13 Jan. 1994; *The Independent,* 13 Jan. 1994; *The Times,* 14 Jan. 1994; *Chronicle* (Guyana), 30 Jan. 1994; *Mirror* (Guyana), 2 Feb. 1994; *The Bookseller,* 11 Feb. 1994; *The Independent,* 24 Feb. 1994; *The Times,* 19 March 1994; *Guardian,* 16 April 1994; *The Independent on Sunday,* 17 April, 1994; *New Statesman,* 22 April 1994; *Guardian,* 23 April 1994; *Daily Telegraph,* 30 April 1994; *Sunday Times,* 8 May 1994; *Scotland on Sunday,* 16 May 1994; *Mirror* (Guyana), 22 May 1994; *The Age* (Melbourne), 25 June 1994; *Big Issue,* June 1994; *Times Literary Supplement,* 23 Sept. 1994; *World Literature Today,* Summer 1995; *Third Text,* Summer 1995.

NOTES ON CONTRIBUTORS

Wolfgang Binder is Associate Professor of American Studies at the University of Erlangen, in Germany. His books include studies of American slave narratives and Hispanic literature. He is a leading German translator of Caribbean writing.

Frank Birbalsingh is Associate Professor of English at the University of York, Toronto, Canada. His books include *Passion and Exile, Essays in Caribbean Literature*, and *Indenture and Exile: The Indo-Caribbean Experience*.

Kwame Dawes is Chairman of the Division of Arts and Letters, University of South Carolina. His doctoral dissertation was on Jamaican fiction. His books include *Prophets* and *Progeny of Air*.

Margery Fee is Associate Professor of English at the University of Calgary, in Alberta, Canada. She has published essays on post-colonial literature.

Kevin Grant read English at Middlesex University and is currently conducting research for a book on Asians in Britain, focusing on the BCCI collapse.

Karen McIntyre is currently completing her doctoral thesis on David Dabydeen's works at the University of Bristol. She teaches at Cheltenham and Gloucester College.

Mark McWatt is Dean of Arts at the University of West Indies (Cave Hill Campus, Barbados). He is editor of *The Journal of West Indian Literature*, and his books include *Interiors* and *The Language of El Dorado*.

Benita Parry is one of Britain's leading post-colonial literary theorists. Her numerous publications include studies on Conrad and on the Anglo-Indian novel.

Jean Popeau's doctoral dissertation at the University of London was on Negritude. He teaches for the Borough of Waltham Forest. He has published on Cuban writing.

Mario Relich teaches for the Open University and is also a free-lance reviewer for the *Scotsman*, *West Africa* and other journals. He has published essays on African and Caribbean culture in a variety of international journals.

Sarah Lawson Welsh graduated from the University of Kent and completed her doctoral dissertation on Caribbean language and literature at the University of Warwick. She teaches at the University of York, England.

INDEX OF NAMES